FROM THE LAND OF PIGS AND INDIANS

TRUST HIM

Dr. Dean Kroeker

outskirts
press

Glossary

Dęni - Indian Tribe
Mura Piraha - Indian Tribe
Paumari - Indian Tribe
Porto Velho - The Old Port
Manaus - Interior Brazilian city
Churrascaria – Brazilian Steak House
Fari – Tribal Chief and dear friend
Karatiana - Indian Tribe
Apurina - Indian Tribe
Belem - Northern Brazilian city
Wycliffe Bible Translators - Huntington Beach, California;
Orlando, Florida
Summer Institute of Linguistics - Dallas, Texas
Jungle Aviation and Radio Service (JAARS) –
Waxhaw, North Carolina
Missionary Aviation Fellowship (MAF) –
Nampa, Idaho
Purus River

Dedication

To my bride for 37 years, and my best friend, Betty (2011).

In acknowledgment to my precious wife and mother of
our children. Betty demonstrated a tenacious commitment
to share God's love by caring for the hidden people in our
world. I admire her ability to "Trust Him" no matter what
was going on in our lives. Out of my love for her and our
family, I have attempted to script some of the experiences
we enjoyed together as a gift to our family, grandchildren
and any one that reads my attempt to record a precious time
in our lives. Many times during the process of scripting
these experiences I had to stop and recover from extreme
agony of missing my bride. Other times, I just broke out
in laughter remembering the situations in which we placed
ourselves. My prayer is that Betty and I leave a legacy of
Hope and Trust in the unfailing love of Jesus.

To Elizabeth Brooks, thank you for sharing your God given
skills crafting the words in this book. Your skill makes it

possible for the reader to grasp the communication intent by the author. And Katia Matter, for conducting the final edit. Through your talents, the following pages come to life.

I appreciate you both!

To the readers, my prayer is that the words and description of our experiences draw you closer to the God that created you, while you were in your mother's womb. May you grasp the incredible truth of how high, wide, deep, and long His love is for YOU! I am opening the door to our lives and invite you to join me as you read some of the experiences my wife and I shared together.

Until we stand together covered in HIS love

In Tribute

To our children:
Duane and Stephanie
Joshua and Sarah
Cheyenne and Alison
Celea and Kyle

And to our grandchildren:
Kayla Kroeker
Kyle Kroeker
Moriah Kroeker
Naomi Kroeker
Lydia Kroeker
Hosanna Kroeker
Shane Hoodman
Linnea Hoodman
Dean Hoodman
Levi Hoodman
*Helena, *dancing with Grandma in Heaven*
Olivia Hoodman

*Shiloh, *dancing with Grandma in Heaven*
*Asa, *dancing with Grandma in Heaven*
*Coniah, *dancing with Grandma in Heaven*
*Noel, *dancing with Grandma in Heaven*
Karis Kroeker
Ruth Kroeker
*Shai, *dancing with Grandma in Heaven*
To my precious family, my prayer is that you allow the
Lord be your guide as you "Trust Him."

I love you ALL,
Dad, Grandpa, Papa

John 5:24-25
Truly, truly, I say to you, whoever hears my word and
believes him who sent me has eternal life. He does not
come into judgment, but has passed from death to life. 25
"Truly, truly, I say to you, an hour is coming, and is now
here, when the dead will hear the voice of the Son of God,
and those who hear will live.

Psalm 50:15
And call upon me in the day of trouble;
I will deliver you, and you shall glorify me.

Isaiah 59:1
Surely the arm of the LORD is not too short to save,
nor his ear too dull to hear.

Psalm 107:19
Then they cried to the LORD in their trouble,
and he delivered them from their distress.

To the Reader

It all began with a series of divine appointments for my wife, Betty, and me as we began our lives together. When we fully discovered Jesus, we committed ourselves to serving our loving heavenly Father to the very best of our abilities. After all, that was the least we could offer Him after He gave His only Son to die for us and to offer us forgiveness. As we started the journey of unabashedly following where the Lord was leading, we discovered how He had made us into exactly who we needed to be for this journey. The abnormal loves in our lives led us on a journey of serving and sharing the love of God to the hidden people of the world.

I think one of the inevitable truths in life is that we are all a little weird inside. We all have odd little likes and preferences that set us apart from the status quo. Whether we like it or not, we are all terribly unique. But why is that something we fight? Why do we hide all of the strange little things that we love deeply – the things that really make our skin itch with excitement? No, I'm not talking about things along the lines of deviance and dishonorable behavior: I'm talking about good, clean, honest oddities.

When you read this book, think about the things that make you different. Think about the things that you like – maybe even love – that make other people scratch their heads and call you crazy. This story, this journey, all started with a man who was obsessed with pigs and a woman who was obsessed with Indians. That's a pretty strange combination if you ask me. But, you know what? That weirdness, those strange loves, are what made this story worth telling. While you experience this journey, think about the ways God has called you to use YOUR own loves. What has he set on your heart that can change the world? How can you do what you love for the Good of humanity? How can you embrace your uniqueness and go conquer the world?

Here is the thing: we are only on this Earth for a moment – a millisecond, really. Why do we waste so much of our time here worrying about what people will say? While we sit around and wait for God to "call" us to something of grand proportions, we waste the real opportunities we have each and every day. Again, embrace what makes you who you really are. Jump into the world weirdness first and go for the journey God has actually called you to. Don't sit around waiting for a sign – just get off your duff and go do *something*. We cannot all be called to the jungle, but we can all make a real difference in the world we live in each and every day. There are hidden people everywhere you look, and they are all in desperate need of hearing the good news of Jesus. Do not waste the opportunities you have today simply because it is not the glamorous mission your ego longs for. Be a missionary at the grocery store, at the DMV, and, if God so calls you, in the middle of the jungle in Brazil. Take those weird little loves your heart has – those pigs and Indians – and actually do something for God's kingdom. Do not waste your weirdness: embrace it.

The pages that follow are samplings of personal experiences Betty and I enjoyed together. Many of the precious lives we had the privilege of taking part in are now rejoicing in the Lord's overwhelming redemptive power. Indigenous churches have been established, medical clinics have been built, and the various languages groups now have schools teaching them how to read and write in their mother tongue. It is my earnest hope that through reading our stories, the Holy Spirit makes it relevant to your own life.

The lyrics written by Terry MacAlmon, "Holy Are You Lord," speak to the desire of my heart as I crafted these words to tell about our time of ministry:

Hear the sound of heaven, like the sound of many waters
It's the sound of worship, coming from the throne
Cries of adoration, as men from every nation
Lift their voice to make His glory known, singing

Holy, holy, holy are you Lord
Holy, holy, holy are you Lord
The elders and angels bow
The redeemed worship you now
Holy, holy, holy are you Lord

Consider this book as a gift from Betty and me as you read the words pouring out of my heart. Betty and I made a commitment to leave behind a legacy that will live on in the hearts of our family and the people they touch. My prayer for you is that as you read these words, the Holy Spirit will touch your heart to care for the hidden people of this world – be it in America or somewhere across the globe.

Dean Kroeker

Table of Contents

Introduction

Dear reader,

As a pastor of 26 years with friends across the country, I'm very often asked to read and comment on things being produced within the context of family and ministry. It's always a joy. However, every now and then something comes across my desk that is beyond "good." The book that you're holding in your hands is one of those rare and pleasant exceptions.

Instead of carving out some time over a couple of weeks to get through the "material," I read the entirety of this work in two settings... only because a family commitment caused me to put it down the first time.

What Dr. Kroeker does in this text is beyond storytelling and teaching. He exposes two streams of powerful and significant human drama. The first stream flows in the direction of a loving Christian household in which husband and wife are so committed to each other and to Christ we can't help but learn and be inspired from watching their interactions. The second is the stream of ministry passion that is not just flowing, it is a volatile set of level five rapids.

The page turning component of this book is fueled by the constant thought, a subtext in my own mind at least, that keeps asking the question, "Are there still people who are willing to do this for the cause of Christ!" If I hadn't seen Dr. Kroeker on campus, if I didn't know him from face-to-face conversation, I might think that these characters were made up and spiritualized for the sake of creating some drama in the readers mind. But, I'm please to tell you these are real people, who really engaged the mission field, because they really love the Lord, and they really made a difference.

It's inspiring and convicting at the same time. Not only did this book cause me to evaluate what I call "sacrifice" in my day today ministry obligations, but I also set the book down to go find my wife and embrace her before we prayed together.

I'm very thankful that this story of a family, a missionary and an incredible adventure has been put on paper. This is something that every Christian leader, minister and serious volunteer should read in hopes that it might give them perspective, call them out, and give them vision that God can do in them more than ever expected.

I'm privileged to have been able to read this, and prayerfully, I am hoping that all subsequent readers will be as encouraged as I.

Andy Addis

1
Where It All Started

My life started in a little Kansas community called Inman.
We lived out in the country, and very seldom did we venture
into town. "Town," if we did go, was about 15 miles away.
Mom made our food, clothes – everything we needed was
in our little microcosm: we did not even have electricity or
indoor plumbing. We didn't need the "outside." If you think
about it, living in the jungle was really just going back to my
roots at a new address.

My dad was always sick with asthma and respiratory issues
when I grew up, so much of our family income went to paying his medical bills. When I got out of high school, I wanted
to get out of that controlled environment. I went to Omaha,
Nebraska – the end of the world for me at the time. I finished a bible degree at a college and immediately moved
to California. It was in those years that my weird likes and

dislikes started to make sense in regards to who I was. I went through a season where I tried my very hardest to sequester myself off from the rest of the world. I found someone to hire me and I petitioned for them to give me the job that paid the least and didn't require me talking to people.

I was, for all intents and purposes, alone in the vast populous that is California – and I wanted it that way.

They gave me exactly what I wanted by tasking me with sweeping out great big 40-45' rental trailers. It is HOT in L.A. and it is HOT in those trailers, but I was totally okay with that. I didn't want to be around people, so if being miserably hot meant being alone, I was fine with that fate. During that time, the office manager saw something in me that I didn't see in myself. He encouraged me – prodded and poked at me – to get into sales. But how do you go into sales when you don't want to talk? How do you sell to people without any verbal interaction?

There was a distinct disconnect in this situation.

Eventually he convinced me to go to lunch with him. Fast forward after consistent attempts to encourage me to get out of my self-inflicted depression, we became friends – close friends, even. After less than a year, I was offered a branch for this company in Denver, Colorado. Me, the young man who wanted to sweep trailers in the sweltering heat of L.A. instead of dealing with people, had now found myself with an offer to be responsible for a significantly large company.

While I was being motivated by this gentleman, I also was in the process of meeting my soon-to-be wife, Betty. For a reason only God himself can provide, I had decided to start going to this church in Long Beach. While attending this congregation, there was a woman there who was dead set on playing matchmaker in my life. She kept poking, pushing, prodding, and irritating me to go to this "singles" group the church had. I, of course, had no interest in being lumped in with the other unfortunate recruits. I had no desire to join this crowd of desperate singles. And yet, a few weeks into her social insistence, I found myself at one of their events.

Thank God I did.

It was there, in this crowd of uncoupled churchgoers that I met my bride.

Now, back to my job offer in Denver, Colorado. I had only known Betty a mere five weeks when this opportunity arose. I knew I wanted to go on this adventure, but I didn't want to go alone. So we got married. We spent our honeymoon moving across the country. How romantic, right? We had this VW van – it was like an old hippie van – and it was great. Our adventure started out in the kind of haphazard, fly-by-the-seat-of-your-pants fashion a love story like ours deserves.

I found myself being quite successful in Denver, working for this company called Rentco. I was out selling some big markets by closing on leases for this company, and I was having a really good time doing so. Well, then God started to talk to us and that's really where our adventure took off.

It was in Denver that we found Jesus in a deep personal relationship. Betty and I had accepted the Lord, but we were so new – we had no idea. In fact, when Betty would read something in scripture that she didn't agree with, she would simply rip it out of her Bible. The gal that led her to Christ (she was a Campus Crusade person) told Betty that what she needed to do was read her Bible every day. She was given a Bible and she started to read. She would read this chapter and go, "Oh, that can't possibly be right!" and she'd rip it out. To this day, I don't know what happened to that Bible, but that Bible had hundreds of pages missing. I'm sure that if I could have stapled those pages together it would have been the essence of the Scripture – because whatever the Lord was asking her to do, she just didn't want to do it.

Here we were, two undeniably headstrong new believers, and it was in this state of flabbergasted belief that we found ourselves on the path that led us to the land of pigs and Indians.

While we were in Denver, we had a spiritual encounter that prepared us for the ministry we would later encounter in Brazil. We started teaching a Special Ed. Class in our local church. There were a lot of kids in that church that needed a little extra attention and we felt compassion towards them – we felt the Lord leading us to help them. They were treated as if they were incapable. They weren't, but that was the general assumption of them. In all honesty, quite a few of them were utterly brilliant – they had other issues that kept them from functioning in a way that society deemed "normal". They could not communicate effectively enough to fit seamlessly into the rest of the world.

It was out of that class that the Lord started to teach us what real ministry is all about. It was also while we were at this church that I became good friends with their Missions pastor and he started talking missions with me, and it was out of that relationship that God called us to Wycliffe Bible Translators/ The Summer Institute of Linguistics.

I went from Kansas, to Nebraska, to Los Angeles, to Denver, and eventually to the Jungle. We went to Brazil because there was a need – a need for someone with the skills that my wife and I had. We found ourselves in the territory of Rhondonia, an interior town – called Porto Velho – very close to a large tributary of the Amazon.

The Amazon essentially became our highway and was how we would get in and out of the different tribal areas. Manaus is the interior city that kind of serves as the hub for the region we were in and that's where we would buy most of our supplies. We would either take our own boat or hire a boat to take material out to the tribal areas.

We lived in five different tribal groups in Brazil, most of which were in the states of Amazonas and Rhondonia. The distance between thee indigenous language groups varied a great deal. They were all relatively accessible: the furthest tribe we worked with was about a five-hour flight out and the nearest was about an hour, but to get there without a plane was incredibly difficult. It took many days to get into several of our locations.

Of course, it had to be this way.

My Missions Pastor friend had warned me about this. He remarked that if it was easy, someone would have already been there. Someone would have already touched the hearts of these people. They would already know about Jesus, but because it was a hot, humid, buggy place, no one had told them.

When I got there, I immediately knew what he meant. It is a hard place to live– there are no comforts in this jungle. But once we were there, it really didn't seem that terrible. Despite all of our hardships, we fell in love with the tropical jungle of Brazil.

We worked out of an area called Porto Velho, which kind of served as the nucleus of our operations. That became the location for us to receive our mail and the location for the translators to access electricity enabling them to do their linguistic and translation work on the computer. It became a refuge for us, a little oasis of comfort in the wildness of the jungle.

The mission was committed to providing a New Testament translation into different indigenous language groups, and we were assigned to work with five distinctly different cultural groups as Community Development Specialists. Our primary goal was to help these tribes learn basic business and medical skills that would enrich their quality of life in order to survive even after we were gone. The size of these groups varied from tribe to tribe, the largest numbering in the thousands and the smallest in the low hundreds.

Living with these tribes often meant our only direct access to the outside came from rivers and water channels. We became very dependent on the water level that changed so drastically between the dry and rainy seasons each year. It was not uncommon for the water to rise and fall over 60', making planting agricultural projects a very tumultuous process.

There is a vast cultural difference between the interior tribes of Brazil and the large, populous cities. International and domestic air travel is well-established in the cities, but out in the jungle is a drastically different story. Time has very little impact on life in the jungle – their whole world is focused entirely on the present.

How can I hunt or fish today so we can eat?

Their entire world is focused on hunting and gathering, and they have little to no contact with the outside world. Their culture is shaped by what it takes for them to survive. When we were assigned to the five groups, we were always located hours and hours away from any major city. There was no access to stores or shops where we could purchase material – we were on our own in the vast amazon jungle.

Looking back, growing up on a farm in mid-Kansas without electricity and very little outside contact was incredibly useful preparation for living in the jungle. Throughout my childhood, we never had the ability to purchase any needed equipment, so my father would create tools and equipment out of discarded material instead of trying to buy new. That became my life-style out there in the jungle of Brazil.

After our first four years living in the Amazon basin, we were given the opportunity to take a six-month furlough and return to the U.S. to retool and take care of medical issues that had come up while we were in the jungle. While we were back in Denver, the Mission Administration asked us to return to the jungle, but we would only be focusing on two – certainly not more than three – tribal locations.

This was an incredible answer to prayer for Betty and me. The first time we went to Brazil, we felt so inadequate when we were trying to make an impact in any of the five different groups we worked with. Not only are the languages different, so are the cultures. Finally, we were given the opportunity to focus on a deeper level of language learning – we could actually develop at least a basic ability to communicate in their "mother tongue."

Limiting our focus to fewer tribes completely changed the relationships with our indigenous families. Betty's influence as a medical professional became much more respected as she taught them on how to care for themselves (and their family) on their own in the future. My ability to teach the tribes about growing food became so much more than the simple classroom learning I had to utilize on our first trip to Brazil. This time, we could plant corn and rice and could see it mature. We harvested the plants and then I taught them how to save seeds so they could repeat the cycle over and over.

Nine years later, after our family had experienced tremendous health and emotional challenges, we were assigned back to the U.S. where we would assume the responsibility of re-cruiting new missionaries to join Wycliffe Bible Translators while we lived and studied in Southern California. After twenty-seven years serving in various areas of responsibil-ity, we retired our commitment to the mission. While we were in Huntington Beach, Betty and I both completed our education. Betty attained two doctorate degrees and I earned my Ed.D. Degree in Organizational Leadership.

Through a series of events, the Lord called us back to Inman, Kansas, where we would begin yet another new chapter in our lives. We found ourselves on a farm very near the one I grew up on 40 years earlier. Even though we were no longer with Wycliffe, Betty continued her mission to help the hid-den people by growing healthy food for the large population of cancer survivors in the area. After a few years together in Inman, the Lord called my Betty home to Him and not a day goes by that I don't long to be reunited with her in Heaven.

99
Betty

While in California, I started attending a church in Long Beach where the pastor's wife believed herself to be a matchmaking aficionado. For weeks, she had been trying to convince me to go to a progressive dinner and in an attempt to finally get her off my back, I reluctantly accepted. At the first stop I ran into a young lady and we immediately hit it off.

There was something about her that I instantly liked.

She was not bashful, but not in an inappropriate way. I could tell she didn't want to be there either. I didn't know this at the time, but – just like me – she had reluctantly decided to attend to get the same matchmaker off her back.

Unwittingly to one another, we had both resigned ourselves to coming to this dinner, but neither of us planned on going only in body. Both of us had decided that if we were going to go, we wouldn't just sit around like a bump on a pickle—we were determined to have fun.

And we certainly did.

Man, this little gal was chock full of energy. She was undeniably happy, but incredibly driven. She was a spitfire. We started to talk and instantly found ourselves lost in deep conversation. I don't remember what we were even eating at that first stop. It didn't matter – we were too engaged in our conversation to waste time eating. Eventually it came time to go to our next stop so I said, "Ride with me."

She rode with me for the rest of the night and five weeks later we were married.

Betty was one happy, compassionate woman. The whole time I was with her on this earth, she was constantly reaching out to help those that were hurting – all the way to the day she died. Even when we moved back to the United States, Betty never stopped reaching out to people. She always said that our mission from Brazil didn't change when we came back to the U.S. "We just changed addresses."

She had a vibrancy for life unmatched by anyone I have ever met. Whether it was working with the Indians of Brazil, helping the homeless of Santa Ana, or growing healthy food for cancer survivors in the middle of Kansas, Betty gave it everything she had. Her passion was relentless.

I was reading some of her poetry the other day – she's not a poet, she's an artist – and her vitality is undeniable. Her poems didn't rhyme like I thought they should, but they possessed this raw beauty that her passion marked everything with.

Oh, and she was funny. She was a Texan and they have their own kind of humor down there, but my, was she funny. If you were in a large room and there was a group laughing, Betty was always in the middle of it. Her jokes were brilliant – sharp, quick, and dripping with wit. Her uncanny ability to find words on the fly is also what made her such an incredible therapist. She had very few clients that only came once – I honestly don't remember any, but there may have been one or two.

She would do some things that were kind of off-the-wall, and she was *always* busy. She had two psychology doctorates and was going after her third when she left this earth. She never ran out of gas until the finish line, so much so that I was completely unprepared for her departure. I thought there was no way she could possibly run out of energy before I did. I'm still caught off guard by it, honestly. No matter how much time passes after her departure, it will always feel like she was with me yesterday.

Once Betty made up her mind on something, there was no room for compromise. How else could we have gotten married in five weeks? How else could we have taken our babies out into the middle of the jungle? She was devastatingly protective of her babies. People knew not to mess with our kids, but she never had to resort to ugly behavior to enact that understanding. She had this uncanny ability to turn absurd situations into something that made complete and total sense – and people felt at ease while she was doing so.

Her vivacious flexibility allowed us to change jungle locations at the drop of a hat. Literally, we could be ready to go somewhere new in a matter of minutes. It didn't matter if we didn't have everything we needed – we figured it out. She simply did not have any time to waste. Instead of waiting for the right time, she shared Jesus like the opportunity had an expiration date. She didn't have the patience to wait until all of the boxes had been checked on her checklist – she knew Jesus was more important than making carefully laid out plans.

She operated under this notion:

*People are more anxious to hear about Jesus
than we are to share.*

And she set her heart on fixing that problem. She knew that people were desperate for the Good News of Jesus and she made up her mind to share it like wildfire.

In so many ways, Betty taught me how to give. I came from a very tight, controlled world and I never learned how to give, but Betty gave to the world spiritually, physically, emotionally, and financially. We were like two raging rivers,

Betty and me. We were both driven and obstinate, and our opposition meant we had to work hard at having a good marriage. This notion that "opposites attract" in a way that fills the holes in each person in a marriage is complete and utter hooey.

Being opposites is *hard*. While there were certainly things about Betty's "opposite" tendencies that I found attractive, there were a lot of times that our opposites turned into opposition. But Betty's tenacity and her joy for life always pushed me to be a better person. She didn't complete me or make me whole – only Jesus can do that – but she helped soften my edges and taught me so much about the abounding, gracious love of our Lord.

I am a huge Denver Broncos fan, and I was slightly obsessed when we lived in Denver. In order to make sure I didn't miss any of the games on TV, I always checked the game times before I decided which church service we would go to on Sundays. We went to a massive church that had multiple services every Sunday, and there was an elaborate system for funneling the people in and out of the sanctuary between services. The sermons couldn't be too long or they would bleed into the next service's time slot and cause a mess. This made it easy for me to map out how much time I needed after church to make it home in time for the game.

Then one Sunday, we had a guest pastor. He preached and preached, completely oblivious to the delicately laid out structure necessary for balancing the fragile ecosystem of multiple services. The longer he talked, the more my watch burned into my skin. My carefully crafted plan was being demolished with every passing minute. Eons after his initial "In conclusion," the sermon was finally over.

Because there were multiple services in immediate succession, the current service would exit through doors at the front of the sanctuary while the people coming for the next service would enter from the back. But the guest pastor was tragically unaware of the system - he invited everyone in the current service to greet him in the back of the sanctuary.

What ensued was a bottleneck of bodies like Los Angeles freeway traffic at 5:00 pm that would make the So. California highway department proud.

Didn't he know I had a game to watch?

Betty had been jabbing my grumpy ribs for quite a while by this point. She knew exactly how frustrated I was, and how precious those Broncos were to me. We escaped the sanctuary and were finally wading through the sea of people to the parking lot when Betty spotted a couple we knew.

And she had the audacity to catch their attention and strike up a conversation.

After a while, I couldn't endure the agony of wasting time any longer. I needed to get home for that game. Didn't Betty know that? I tried to convince the couple that they needed to hurry into the sanctuary or else they wouldn't be able to find a seat. Of course, my attempt completely flopped. On and on, the conversation continued.

Finally, I just couldn't take it anymore. I had to get out of there. So, I interjected into the conversation a carefully crafted statement. "It was great to see you guys, but we have to go."

And I headed towards the car.

I didn't get very far before I noticed that Betty wasn't coming with me. She knew exactly how much I loved those Broncos and how important watching the game was to me, and yet she stayed put. I sat in the car and fumed until she finally made her way out there. Even after we finally got home, I continued to fume. Lunch came around and I was still too mad to eat.

I went directly to our den, closed the door, and turned on the TV to watch one of the most boring games I had ever seen. Mid-sulk, the Holy Spirit profoundly confronted my attitude. I realized how wrong I was, and how I had publicly embarrassed myself, my wife, and our friends.

I went to my sweet Betty and told her how sorry and wrong I was. She had known this all along, of course, but she patiently waited for me to come to that conclusion on my own. That was my Betty: fiery, obstinate, and unwaveringly gracious. She always pushed me to be a better person, even when I was frustrated with her for misguided reasons.

She never ran out of patience – not with the Indians, not even with me.

Psalms 139: 1-18

O Lord, You have searched me and known me.
You know when I sit down and when I rise up; You under-
stand my thought from afar.
You scrutinize my path and my lying down,
And are intimately acquainted with all my ways.
Even before there is a word on my tongue,
Behold, O Lord, You know it all.
You have enclosed me behind and before,
And laid Your hand upon me.
Such knowledge is too wonderful for me;
It is too high, I cannot attain to it.
Where can I go from your Spirit?
Or where can I flee from Your presence?
If I ascend to heaven, You are there;
If I make my bed in Sheol, behold, You are there.
If I take the wings of the dawn,
If I dwell in the remotest part of the sea,
Even there Your hand will lead me,
And Your right hand will lay hold of me.
If I say, "Surely the darkness will overwhelm me,
And the light around me will be night,"
Even the darkness is not dark to You,
And the night is as bright as the day.
Darkness and light are alike to You.
For You formed my inward parts;
You wove me in my mother's womb.

I will give thanks to You, for I am fearfully
and wonderfully made;
Wonderful are Your works,
And my soul knows is very well.

My frame was not hidden from You,
When I was made in secret,
And skillfully wrought in the depths of the earth;
Your eyes have seen my unformed substance;
And in Your book were all written
The days that were ordained for me,
When as yet there was not one of them.
How precious also are Your thoughts to me, O God!
How vast is the sum of them!
If I should count them, they would outnumber the sand.
When I awake, I am still with You.

999
A Call to Wycliffe

Right after Betty and I got married, we moved from Southern California to Denver, Colorado. We spent our ever-so-romantic honeymoon moving our lives across the country in order to start a brand-new adventure. I had received an offer from my employer, Fruehauf Trailer Rental Company – Rentco, to transfer to Denver and assume the position of branch manager for a freight trailer rental company. Betty was in the process of completing her Master's degree in medical surgery, so she transferred from California State University Long Beach to the University of Colorado. In order for us to take the opportunity to begin our married life together in Denver and for her to finish her Master's program, we arranged our work to accommodate each other's schedules.

Now we found ourselves not only trying to get to know each other as a married couple, but also learning how to function in our new jobs and responsibilities. Betty was thriving at the University of Colorado and I was finding some success opening new markets in Salt Lake City, El Paso, and Albuquerque – the Lord was blessing my occupational efforts with some pretty big contracts. During this time of transition, the Lord started to work inside of us, but in very different ways. I found myself becoming terribly interested in hogs and Betty becoming increasingly fascinated with Indians. We became so enamored with our new interests that it started to pull us apart, so much so that our friends shared with us individually that we were both *obsessed*.

I found a hog ranch about 10 miles from the office where I would take my lunch break and just go sit with the pigs to enjoy their presence. While I enjoyed my daily task of basking in the glory of hog farming, Betty began expressing her distaste for my new obsession. She told me she didn't like pigs, that they *stink*. Naturally, I was grievously offended that she would speak so poorly of something I so dearly loved.

While my lunchtime romance with the pig farm continued, Betty's attraction to Indians intensified. We watched every movie that had "Indian" in the titles – we watched anything that even *hinted* at having Indians in it. She voraciously read every book she found that related to Indians. Of course, I was not nearly as excited about Indians as she was – she was *obsessed*, after all. My response to her Indians was certainly as offensive as the disdain she showed for my pig habit.

All of this tension started to really stress our marriage. The more I liked pigs, the more Betty was repulsed by the thought of buying a hog ranch. The more obsessed she got with Indians (inappropriately so, I thought), the more I resisted going to see another Indian movie. We were completely at odds, and it seemed like maybe both of us were too stubborn to ever consider giving up our obsessions.

I remember coming home from work one afternoon. I barely made it in the door, hadn't even had a chance to greet my lovely wife, when Betty said, "Dean, have you been out to that hog ranch again?" Apparently, when I was out having lunch with the pigs, the aroma penetrated my clothes and my car. She could smell it and she wasn't happy about it. They *repulsed* her.

Our situation did not improve with time. One Sunday morning, we found ourselves having a major discussion – more like an argument. I had just found out about a hog ranch available in Western Kansas, and I intended to buy it. To me, it had huge potential financially and would allow me to live out my dream of raising my most special animal: hogs. But instead of hopping onto my dream train, Betty doubled down on her desire to work with Indians. We were driving to church, "discussing" things, when we stopped at a red light.

Completely exasperated, I started to pray out loud. "Lord, will you please show us if we should purchase this hog ranch or if we should work with Indians?"

It was a terrifying prayer. I already knew that the Lord answered prayer, but this time I had audibly and verbally committed myself to hear the voice of the Lord.

We continued on to church that Sunday morning and sat through the sermon where the pastor gave us no indication of God's will concerning pigs and Indians. Our church had televised this sermon in particular and after the cameras were down, the pastor asked everyone to have a seat. He had an announcement to make. "I want you to meet a special friend of this church community, a missionary we have supported for many years."

Visiting the church that Sunday morning was a missionary from Brazil. She was in Denver to assist in the dedication of a single-engine Cessna 206. A group of friends living in the Denver area had been involved in raising funds to purchase this plane, something they'd been working on for many long years. We didn't really know very many missionaries at that point, and since we were still new to our church, we definitely didn't know this one. The pastor then announced that this lady would be the speaker at a ladies' luncheon the very next day.

I was scheduled to leave for Salt Lake City to conduct a large sales presentation, and the importance of this meeting meant I felt justified in flying out Sunday afternoon so I could get settled in at the hotel and finish prepping for my meeting on Monday. If I'm being honest, leaving Sunday was very intentional on my part. I needed to get out of there before the Lord gave us some sort of indication that we should work with Indians.

Of course, when Betty heard the announcement at church that Sunday, she quickly rearranged her plans so she could go to the luncheon. She was ecstatic to hear this missionary from Brazil. When she was sitting at the luncheon listening to the missionary, Betty became highly aware that she was using terms like: tribes, translations, community development work, and so on – all the words that made Betty's Indian-loving heart beat faster.

After the presentation, when all of the other ladies had moved on to enjoy their lunch, Betty felt compelled to get up and speak to the missionary. Instead of sitting and enjoying her lunch like everyone else, she excused herself from the table and introduced herself to Joyce Abrahamson. In her upfront and direct manner, Betty said, "Joyce, can I ask you a question and will you promise not to laugh?"

With a tremble in her voice she asked, "Do you by any chance need a hog farmer to work with the Indians in Brazil?"

Immediately, Joyce shouted, "YES! We have been praying for five years that the Lord would call someone to come to Brazil to work with the Indians and share their skills and knowledge of how to work with pigs!"

Rather abruptly, Betty excused herself from the luncheon and called me. I was rather upset when the hotel manager strolled into the conference room during my meeting and said, "Dean, there is a call for you from Denver. It's your wife."

Betty should have known better. She knew how important this meeting was and she knew how intense I got when I was working on a big sales presentation. Once my initial shock wore off, I realized that whatever she was calling about must have been really important if she was willing to interrupt my meeting for it.

As I excused myself from the meeting I started to get worried: why on earth would she be calling me in the middle of a Monday unless there was some kind of emergency?

I picked up the phone and Betty unloaded what had just transpired during her luncheon.

With absolutely no hesitation, I told her, "Find out everything you can about this mission agency. Who is Wycliffe? What kind of organization are they? How do we contact them to start the process of moving to Brazil?"

———

We had no clue about the requirements to join Wycliffe Bible Translators. In fact, we knew absolutely nothing about them. We had no idea we would need to be accepted as members before we could ever go on an assignment. We didn't know we would be required to attend the Summer Institute of Linguistics training in Oklahoma City before we would ever be considered for an assignment to Brazil.

But even with all of that, we weren't deterred.

After coming back to Denver later in the week, we immediately got in touch with a real estate agent and put our house on the market. We were moving to Brazil.

———

When we make a commitment to follow where the Lord's leading us, that doesn't necessarily mean that the road is going to be smooth and straight. Betty and I had all kinds of problems to confront.

We had to raise our own financial support. Wycliffe missionaries didn't receive any kind of salary, so we would have to depend on churches and individuals willing to commit to supporting our ministry. While we were jumping headfirst into our Brazil journey, we had also just adopted a child from Vietnam, and we hadn't completed the final legalization process for his citizenship yet.

On top of all of this, we were also heavily involved with teaching a Sunday School class. It was made up of individuals who had special needs and we had all become very emotionally connected to one another. It was going to be really hard to give that up for this new journey.

During this time of rapid transition, Betty and I would often remind each other that before we were born, while we were still in our mother's wombs, God had created us with our unique loves: mine for hogs and Betty's for Indians.

For you formed my inward parts;
You wove me in my mother's womb.
I will give thanks to You, for I am fearfully and
wonderfully made;
Wonderful are Your works,
And my soul knows it very well.
My frame was not hidden from You,
When I was made in secret,
And skillfully wrought in the depths of the earth;
Your eyes have seen my unformed substance;
And in Your book were all written
The days that were ordained for me,
When as yet there was not one of them.
How precious also are Your thoughts to me, O God!
How vast is the sum of them!
If I should count them, they would outnumber the sand.
When I awake, I am still with You.

IV

Summer Institute of Linguistics, SIL

After we applied to serve as Wycliffe missionaries, they required us to complete cross-cultural ministry training, including a number of courses in linguistics. We attended a nine-week program offered at the University of Oklahoma in Norman called the Summer Institute of Linguistics (SIL). Due to budget limitations, Wycliffe Bible Translators (WBT) utilized low-cost dormitories and classroom space on campus.

I will never forget how miserably hot and humid the Oklahoma weather is in summertime. We had two babies in diapers while we were there and, on top of being crammed into a tiny dorm, we also had all of our meals served in a common dining area shared by everyone. We would spend all day in classes while our babies were in daycare, only to crowd into a dining hall to try and have some semblance of family time while we ate. Our kids were so terribly hot and sticky that sitting in a raucous cafeteria hardly felt like peace.

Obviously, it would have been a lot easier to just visit the campus for a weekend, but we were dead set on completing all of the requirements to join Wycliffe Bible Translators. After completing our first four weeks, our joy in that mission had started to wane. It was hard to be excited about our mission with two hot, fussy babies and a tiny dorm room for our home.

Our babies were still taking bottles, so I would wait until around 10 PM – just before the dining hall closed – and go down to get fresh milk for their bottles, and maybe even a light snack for Betty and me during the night. Our room didn't have any air conditioning, and we just had the standard college dorm furniture: two bunk beds, a dresser, and one tiny closet. Because it was so incredibly hot, the milk would usually curdle within two or three hours of getting it from the cafeteria. Our babies would cry for milk through the night, but we had to make them wait until we could get fresh milk when the dining hall opened up again at 6 AM.

It was a terrible and difficult time, but it was wonderful all the same.

We felt God's affirmative call to a ministry in Brazil, a place where the weather would be even more miserably hot and humid than what we experienced in Norman over the summer.

Finally, after we successfully completed the SIL training, we were approved to proceed to our first assignment: jungle camp in Mexico, operated by Wycliffe Bible Translators who were headquartered in Huntington Beach, California.

We were so ready to move on to the ministry that the Lord had so clearly called us to fulfill but the process was moving so slowly…you may be encountering this same issue, desiring the Lord to move much faster, but may I encourage you with the passage from Lamentations 3:25-26: *The Lord is good to those whose hope is in him, to the one who seeks him; it is good to wait quietly for the salvation of the Lord.*

V
Jungle Training Camp

Wycliffe Bible Translator members were required to successfully complete a six-month jungle training experience. This
training was divided into two parts: Level One consisted of
learning survival skills at a jungle base in Southern Mexico
and Level Two was about learning how to implement the
classroom learning through a real-life survival experience in
the jungle with very limited equipment and material.

Betty and I were both excited for this experience. I had grown
up on a farm in Kansas and didn't have indoor plumbing until
I was in middle school – living a basic lifestyle wasn't threat-
ening to me in the slightest. Betty was flooded with a spirit of
anticipation because she loved to be outdoors, and she especially enjoyed camping in primitive places. I remember the
day that we left Dallas, Texas to fly to Mexico where we were
then transported to the location called "base camp." That trip

was filled with all kinds of eagerness and anticipation – and a rather healthy dose of anxiety about what we were getting ourselves into.

Our time at the camp was incredibly structured. There were about 40 or 50 of us new trainees, along with a staff of 10 or 12 missionaries, and all of us were at the camp to learn how to live in a community. For a lot of us, we'd never experienced anything like this before in our entire lives. We shared every single meal together. Luckily, we did have a cook, but it was up to us to appoint shifts to set the table, serve, clean up, and take care of various other duties. Most of us had small children, so there was a daycare facility on site. On top of pitching in at mealtime, members and new trainees who were parents were often asked to help staff the daycare.

While we were at the camp, we were given basic survival training: survival techniques, foods that you can and can't eat in the jungle, fish you shouldn't eat, and so on. After completing the first level of training, Mission Aviation Fellowship was contacted to fly us to an airstrip located near Guatemala. We lovingly referred to this place as "advance base."

We were ecstatic the morning we finally boarded our plane to fly out to advance base: we had been looking forward to this day for months. We knew that the training we were about to get was an invaluable experience that would help us survive living in the jungle of Brazil.

Our flight out was pretty short, and then we literally landed in the middle of a jungle. You couldn't even really see the airstrip until we descended from 5000 feet to maybe 2,000-1,500 feet. We plunked down onto this tiny grass airstrip, got out of the plane, and were instructed to follow the trail and hike to our advance base camp.

After all of the shuttle flights had been completed and all of the trainee groups had arrived, we had our first training meeting. Our classroom consisted of simple tiered seating carved into the side of a hill, and the staff wasted no time on instructing us about what we were about to experience on this adventure. Each family was given a 10' x 10' sheet of blue plastic and a ¾" stove plate. On a daily basis, they told us to be prepared for a survival hike that we would be called to at any point, completely unannounced.

My first task at the camp was to build a house for my family. All I had been given was the stove plate and a piece of plastic. We'd been instructed to bring our machetes and canteens, and I had also brought my little first aid kit, matches, about 20 feet of fish string, and a couple of hooks hanging on my canteen belt.

At about 8:30 the next morning, we all heard a bell – kind of like a cowbell – that signaled us to go on down to the classroom. They gave each family a small food allotment: one pound of rice, a can of pineapple, and a potato for each member of the family. I became very thankful that we had two kids because this meant we got two extra potatoes.

Before they let us get back to work on constructing our little homes – my plastic jungle kingdom – they told us that every morning at 8:30 we would have a three- to four-hour class. We had a lot to learn about how to stay alive in the jungle in case we ever found ourselves all alone, completely isolated from any contact with the outside world. We had to figure out how to survive.

Finally, they let us go back to constructing our shelters. I went back to the location I had selected to build the Kroeker residence. I thought I was rather brilliant: I'd selected a site that was on a hill because the rainy season had already started. Since it was raining every day – all day and night – there was an astonishing amount of water everywhere. I didn't want to be living in a swamp, so I went out and cut some large branches – more like trees, really – to create somewhat of a frame for our little house. I cut some smaller branches to serve as rafters for our roof and I put up the plastic.

I was pretty proud of myself. I had gotten a shelter put up, so now I needed to go ahead and build us a mud stove out of jungle floor clay, which I could place the stove plate on so we could have a fire to use for cooking. I planned on either fishing or hunting to supplement our meager pound of rice, because I did not anticipate our rations lasting too long. I was excited to try my handyman skills out on building this stove. I was building it based upon photos I had seen before, but I had never actually built one of these things before. It was not hard to find the clay, and with the rain pouring down so hard, the clay was soft and easily molded into the shape I needed to build my stove.

Overall, our shelter was rather delightful other than one thing: we didn't have a bed. I went back into the jungle – which was literally all around us – and sought out some small seedlings to thatch a bed. I gathered as many as I could find that were ½ inch in diameter and straight as possible, then proceeded to cut them and weave them into a sleeping pallet. My plan was to build it with a little bit of flexibility so it wouldn't be too hard to sleep on with our sleeping bags. They actually worked well. The only problem we had was getting out of bed. It was hard to climb out of bed without sliding right down the hill because the rain would come down so hard during the night that there would be gushing water going through our shelter by morning.

Eventually, everyone started to get adjusted to our little routines. We'd go down to the training area every morning at the same time: we already knew when the bell was going to ring. Everybody found themselves starting to relax in our little microcosm, and my little family was no exception. There were a couple of days that I forgot my belt with the canteen, machete, and first aid supplies. I remember sitting in class, silently terrified of being woefully unprepared if we were called on our hike that day. Luckily, they waited a while before calling us on our survival hike.

We were coming into the third week of camp and neither the men nor the ladies had been called for the survival experience. We had discovered a good fishing spot down by the lake that was close to the training site. We thought we were doing okay with the food we were eating out of the jungle – we were following instructions on the "safe" food to eat. But even with all of our precautions and carefulness, our family started to experience some health issues.

Our babies contracted typhoid. They were still in diapers, which obviously caused a lot of issues when it came to dealing with the side effects of typhoid. The staff later told us that the Kroeker family set a record for the number of dirty diapers produced while at advance base.

———

We kept on living our lives at the camp and continued our routine of going to training each morning. One morning, we all gathered for a quick devotional before our training session when the director of our base giddily stood up in front of the class and jovially said, "Gentlemen, today is the day for our long-awaited survival hike. Follow me to the canoes – we are leaving right now."

Sure enough, several of the guys had forgotten their machete belts and first aid equipment that day. They weren't allowed to go back and get their supplies: they had to survive without their much-needed equipment. I felt sorry for them. As luck would have it, several of them were the same individuals that were already struggling with existing without the luxuries of first-world American living.

We all piled into our large dugout canoe. It had an outboard motor and was very tippy – it's wobbliness creating a mix of dread and excitement within us. There were 15 of us in the canoe and the powers that be decided we needed to be divided into two teams. We had to randomly call out "1-2" as we coasted down the lake for what seemed like miles.

Finally, we got to the side of the lake. They told all of the 1's to get out. "This is where you will now survive for the next three days and nights. After that, we'll provide you a limited amount of food. But for these next three days and nights, you must exist simply with whatever you can find to eat in the jungle."

I was on team number 1.

The second group stayed in the canoe and we heard them quietly float away. We could see them being taken all the way over to the other side of the lake. It was a big lake and crossing the distance between sides was going to be a long and difficult hike, which I had a feeling we would be doing in the course of the next few days.

I again found myself tasked with building a shelter, except this time I didn't have any plastic for my roof. However, they did teach us how to build an emergency shelter out of jungle material with nothing but a machete. It was actually fun to build this little shelter. I was proud of my work and wished I could take a picture of it, but there was no camera hanging from my machete belt.

This particular area of the jungle was especially primitive. Since I had such success with building my bed at camp, I decided to try and repeat my efforts – only this time I only had to make one big enough for just me because I was all alone.

I was quite enjoying my solitude.

I was starting to understand and appreciate the importance of spending quality time with Jesus and this felt like a perfect opportunity. We were banned from speaking to one another for the next three days. Granted, this was really a non-issue. We were all so isolated that we couldn't even see each other. They told us to move somewhere remote, but where we still felt safe. I remember feeling a sense of security while I was there – I knew Jesus was right there with me in the Mexican jungle.

I did my best to survey the area I was in and be wise about where I put my makeshift home for the next couple of days, and I was especially aware that I needed to stay far away from ant and termite hills. They instructed us that if we happened to run into someone else from our group we weren't allowed to say anything to one another: we had to be totally silent. I suspected that they were doing this to test our limits, to show us how isolated we could be before we would break.

I know that the staff member that was with us was watching for warning signs of extreme emotional duress. Thank goodness they did because someone did end up breaking down. They took care of him, of course, but seeing his despair really brought a new awareness to how much we could handle out there in the wilderness. We started to understand what our limits of survival actually were.

Some of us were enjoying our time in the quietness of the jungle, while other men found the loneliness stifling and iso-lating, I found it to be peaceful, serene almost. But, as nice as it was to catch my breath in nature, I sure enjoyed that little sack of granola and tiny pouch of coffee they gave us after our first three days.

On the fourth day they fished all of us out of seclusion and gathered all of the members of Team #1. The staff guide started laying out what we needed to do next: "Your assign-ment is to find group 2 – they've been over on the other side of the lake. You are responsible for finding them and for reconnecting. They've also been given directions, but we aren't going to share what those are with you."

The gauntlet had been thrown: *Had we been listening? Had we been learning? Had we been absorbing the training they'd given us so far?*

We knew we needed a leader. We had to find some structure to our group if we were going to survive this adventure in one piece. But how were we going to find our way to the oth-er side of the lake? We didn't even have a compass. There's no way we could just walk on the beach to the other side: it was a horridly treacherous mountainous kind of terrain.

After some deliberation and careful consideration, we picked a leader and decided on a game plan. We were going to hike for two hours, rest for 15 minutes, and get right back to hiking for another two hours. It worked fine for the first couple of hours, but then that dastardly beast called human nature kicked in. Some of us were convinced we were walking in circles; some of us thought we were surely headed in the wrong direction. Some of us decided we needed to abandon our plan, that they were going to come and look for us. They wanted to sit down, build a fire, and create some shelters so we could get out of the rain and cold.

It was a trying experience. Inside my head, I wanted to keep going because I was convinced that the instructions they gave us had a purpose. All we needed to do was go find group number two, which we certainly couldn't do if we stopped and made a camp. Our leader was feeling conflicted amidst all of the dissension, but we finally came to a compromise.

We hiked for another two days before we finally found the jungle signal.

The staff had taught us specific survival techniques to survive in daily jungle training classes. When you find yourself lost in the jungle with no idea where you're going but you want to be able to find your way back, just cut a little bit of bark on one side of a tree. Keep marking on either the right or the left, but be consistent about which side you pick, and make yourself a trail detailing where you'd been. We spotted one of these tree signals and we knew we were finally on the right track. All we had to do was follow the markings and we would find our other group.

At last, we found them.

They'd been instructed to mark a trail for us that didn't exceed 500m from where they were located – that was the trail we'd stumbled upon. What a wonderful reunion it was! It was like we were family now. We'd survived base camp together, and now we were survivors of a very real, incredibly challenging experience in the desolate isolation of the jungle.

Several weeks passed before they made the announcement again. It was the ladies' turn.

Our kids were still awfully sick. They were weak and weary and I was uneasy about their mama leaving them to go on a survival hike. Now it was just me and them, and it was wholly up to me to try and feed them.

What do you even feed a child with typhoid when you're in the jungle and don't have a supermarket to go to? You can't just run to the store to get something that will give them a little relief. Needless to say, I was not excited about Betty leaving me for her hike.

The ladies all prepared to start on their survival adventure. I'd already shared my experience with Betty, but, right as they were heading down to get into their canoes, they told the ladies their experience would be completely different than the men. So much for the private plan of action we had worked out together!

My heart sank. I had done my best to prepare Betty for what to expect and now all of that was moot. She was on her own and I was worried about her. I ceaselessly prayed for Betty, that she would come to us in one piece and that we could survive without her. I had a distinct sense in my spirit that Betty was experiencing difficulties out there in the jungle. I think the kids cried each night she was not there. I did my best to comfort them, but I just wasn't their mom. Our bond had become incredibly strong, so totally different than in our first year of marriage.

The ladies had been out for almost a week and they were still requiring all of us men to attend class every morning. Most of us weren't wearing our survival belts anymore. We knew our survival experience was already over, so we didn't see a point in being religious about wearing them any longer.

After one of our morning classes, the camp director stopped me and asked if we could talk. He told me to sit down and wasted no time jumping into what he needed to say. "Your wife has become terribly ill and we have to bring her out of the jungle. We've already contacted Missionary Aviation Fellowship and have requested that they bring us a plane. We need to fly her back to base camp. I don't have any other details, but I needed to let you know that we're prepping for an evacuation."

I was devastated.

I just wanted to be able to talk to her, to comfort her, to be with her.

We didn't even have a radio to talk to each other with. I didn't know what was going on. Did she cut herself with a machete? I doubted it because her technique was too good for such an accident – she had fantastic survival skills.

My mind was racing. The next hour felt like an eternity, but finally the canoe showed up carrying my sweet Betty.

She had an extremely high fever and was hallucinating.

I'd already grabbed all of our belongings – not that we had much. I packed up all of our clothing that had been washed and all of the diapers that had been cleaned.

We walked to the airstrip. It was a long trek, especially with Betty in tow on a stretcher. We sat there and waited for our plane to land on the tiny airstrip. Our jungle pilots were incredibly skilled: they fly by what's called *visual flight rules.* There isn't a tower to guide them, so they have to follow their instincts. They watch rivers and use their internal sense of knowing where they're at.

But on this day, the midmorning clouds moved in and the rain started to pour. It rained and rained and rained while we sat there at the end of our little airstrip. In order to use visual flight rules, you have to be able to see the ground, otherwise there's no feasible way to know where you're at.

So, I sat and waited while the seconds and minutes seemed to slow down to a crawl.

I sat there on a bucket while the rain kept coming right on down while Betty laid there in her stretcher on the ground. We didn't have a bed – we didn't even have a bench. One of the staff members had come to sit with her. She sat down on the muddy ground and held her hand, trying to comfort her in any way possible.

And we just sat there and prayed:

Father, won't you just please open a break in the clouds so the pilot can see the airstrip? PLEASE FATHER!

After waiting and waiting, I finally heard the plane. What beautiful music to our ears! But there was still a heavy cloud cover right over the strip. The director and I begged the Lord:

Please, Father, won't you open a window and allow the pilot to see us? Let him poke through that cloud and land so we can load my bride and get her to a medical facility in Mexico.

The ladies had received similar instructions to my own on their survival hike. They had to make it through those first three days with no provisions other than what they had on their bodies when they left advance base. After two days, Betty started getting incredibly hungry and decided to try and catch some fish. She took her little fish line and hook to one end of a fallen tree and threw it out, but all she caught was minnows. She wasn't getting anything significant enough to actually sustain her. Eventually she got so hungry that she decided she had to do something else – she needed to adapt in order to survive.

She knew that there were usually snails at the bottom of the trees, so she assumed there would be some in the bottom of the lake that had fallen off the trees. She jumped to dive into the water and feel around on the bottom of the floor to see if she could find any.

Remember that Betty is not easily distracted nor has any tendency to submit to defeat.

She knew what happened when you eat a snail, so she cooked them in her canteen. She cooked and cooked them – beyond the required time – like we had been taught in our survival classes. Apparently, she didn't cook it long enough, though, because she was now suffering from a severe case of food poisoning. By the time she made it to the airstrip, she was completely and totally dehydrated.

There we were, sitting on our airstrip, waiting for the plane circling above us. I was praying to my heavenly Father, who I knew intellectually, but at the same time I was experiencing emotional abandonment. It felt like He didn't care about my crying babies – I was crying, too, and Betty didn't have anything left in her to even muster a tear. It felt like I was praying into thin air.

The staff trainer just sat there holding Betty's hand, praying. I could see her lips moving, but I couldn't hear any sound. For the first time in my life, I saw someone praying in the spirit. She was praying words that couldn't be uttered in her own strength.

In that moment of utter despair, God answered our prayers with a miracle. It was like we were watching a video: the clouds opened right in front us. We had specifically asked for a hole in the clouds to open so the plane could see the landing strip, and that is exactly what happened. It felt like Jesus himself was parting the clouds, perfectly timed with the plane's positioning in the sky.

The pilot nosedived through his opening and glided down onto the airstrip.

We hurriedly loaded Betty, our babies, and our few meager possessions. We slammed the doors shut and immediately took back off into heavy clouds that were dumping tons of heavy rain on the jungle floor.

By the time we approached main base, the clouds had lifted and the thunderstorm had run its course, letting us land without a hitch. They'd already made radio contact with the nurse ahead of time, so they were already prepped for Betty when we touched the ground. A gurney had been moved out to the airstrip and the IV drip setup was in place and waiting for us to lift her out of the plane.

After a few very tense days, Betty started to regain her strength. They let us fly back out to the city and get some additional medical assistance at a facility that was equipped with the appropriate medical systems and qualified doctors. Not only had God miraculously protected my bride's life, but He had also provided for me in a way I had never before experienced: I learned how to trust in Him in a very real, very tangible way.

If today you are facing a trial or a challenge that feels completely impossible, I encourage you to trust in the Lord with all of your heart. It might be physical death you or a loved one are facing, a financial crisis, a relationship crisis – whatever – don't try to figure it out all on your own.

Know that our God is a loving God and that He will not abandon you in this hard time. Take some time and reflect on the promises provided for us in the Scriptures.

Proverbs 3: 5-6
Trust in the Lord with all your heart and lean not on your own understanding. In all your ways submit to him, and He will make your paths straight.

Psalms 147:3
He heals the brokenhearted and binds up their wounds.

Proverbs 4:20- 22
My son, give attention to my words; Incline your ear to my sayings. Do not let them depart from your sight; Keep them in the midst of your heart. For they are life to those who find them and health to all their body.

Isaiah 53:4-5
Surely our griefs He Himself bore, and our sorrows He carried; yet we ourselves esteemed Him stricken, smitten of God, and afflicted. But He was pierced through for our transgressions, He was crushed for our iniquities; the chastening for our well-being fell upon Him, and by his scourging we are healed.

VI
Belem

I will never forget leaving Denver for the jungle. After a wonderful commissioning service at our home church in Denver, Colorado, we said goodbye to our precious friends – our special ed. class, who were trying their best to say good-bye through tons of tears and LONG hugs, and the allies we loved so deeply who'd promised to support us and to pray for us during our time in Brazil. We went home that night to sleep, a nearly impossible task. Our excitement and joy – the sheer anticipation of this Great Unknown – was too stimulating to ever make sleep a reality.

We got up early so that our friend could take us to the Denver airport. Our schedule had us flying from Denver to Miami, where we would board a flight on a Brazilian airline that flew us to Belem, Brazil, located on the northeast part of the country. If you have flown commercial flights in the U.S., you're probably quite familiar with the extensive safety presentation. You know how it goes: the flight attendant gives safety instructions or – if your flight is really fancy – they turn on an actual video. As expected, we had become very accustomed to this standard procedure. But today, we were on a Brazilian airline.

I suspect they were giving the exact same safety instructions as the American airlines, but we could not understand a single word of it because the whole flight instruction demonstration was entirely in Portuguese. For all we knew, they could have been selling us Tupperware while the flight crew got the plane ready for takeoff.

It's pretty common for international flights to fly at night, which is how it was for this one. We flew through the night and early into the next morning before we finally landed. When we were finally on the ground, we were greeted by a sight I was hardly prepared to see: our plane was surrounded as soon as it was taxied to the gate with military guards clutching their machine guns as they positioned themselves around our plane before we could exit the aircraft. We had landed in a military-controlled country with very few individual civil rights.

I had a sinking, dreadfully anxious feeling. I couldn't speak Portuguese and had never been to this part of Brazil. I had a sneaking suspicion that there wouldn't even be a representative from Wycliffe Bible Translators there to greet us – the kind of friendly face we desperately needed to counteract the shock of machine-gun-clad guards.

Surprisingly, going through customs was rather uneventful. We had made prior arrangements for a shipment of some of our material things to come later on a boat, so all we had with us was our family and suitcases. We went through customs without any issues: they asked an abundance of questions about the information forms I had completed prior to landing, but I had made sure all of our passports and entry forms were in order. We proceeded right on through the gate, and sure enough, there was a family there to greet us, holding up a little sign that said *Kroeker*.

What a joyous sight it was to see those kind faces waiting for us, ready to make us feel loved and welcomed. I was reminded of the scriptural passage in Matthew 19:29, *And everyone who has left houses or brothers, or sisters or father or mother or wife or children or fields for my sake will receive a hundred times as much.* Our new comrades took us to the Wycliffe Center, which was the location where the translators would work with the language data they gathered while they were in tribal areas. There was a support staff stationed to teach at an American school for the missionary kids and it felt like a miniature American city: a little slice of home in the heart of the jungle.

Our mission provided eight tiny apartments right on the "Center" that we could live in for the next 2-3 months while we got our bearings in this new place. But we had made a commitment while we were attending the Summer Institute of Linguistics in Norman, Oklahoma: we were going to fully submerge ourselves into the Brazilian language and culture at our first opportunity. Instead of living in a socially safe place filled with like-minded missionaries, we opted to look for an apartment in a Brazilian community, preferably one that had no other missionaries within a mile or so of it.

This decision, albeit a rather terrifying one, would force us to speak Portuguese – we would have to stumble along in conversation with our new neighbors. We also decided to explore a lot of fun things on our own without the safety net of waiting for more experienced missionaries to give us guided tours or offer us advice on where or where not to go. We just wanted to discover sights and sounds that connected to our passion and vision on our own.

It didn't take very long for us to become relatively familiarized with riding the city buses – the main mode of transportation for many Brazilians. In Brazil, only the wealthy upper class have the money to buy cars. We were not nearly so prestigious: we lived in an apartment complex with multiple homes bursting with families and children, which was located within walking distance of the Center.

Our first Brazilian assignment was to complete a Portuguese course, so we got to sit in class every morning – five days a week – while we worked through a textbook called *How to Communicate in Portuguese.* Here's the thing about learning: everyone has different learning styles and methods that seem to be more conducive to their own way of thinking and learning. For me, sitting in a classroom for five days a week, trying to get a grasp on the grammatical construction of the Portuguese language was incredibly difficult. It was a real challenge to focus on textbook fill-in-the-blanks while the instructor was attempting to motivate us to learn. Not only did she have a real challenge with us, but she was also working from the position of being blind and could not see us walking around the room while she was working on intonation, conjugation, tonal recognition, etc.

I wanted to get out – to interact with the Brazilians face to face. I wanted to practice the phrases I was learning in real life, and I wanted to get past those initial faux-conversational phrases we started with as fast as possible. While "Onde esta agência do correio" (Where's the post office?),

"instalações sanitárias" (Where's the bathroom?), or "Onde esta da cozinha" (Where's the kitchen?) are all important self-preservation phrases to learn, I wanted to get into the meat of the language. Portuguese seemed like such a beautiful language and I quickly grew tired of subliminal phrases – I wanted to start the real, emotional communication, "Eu querer fala em português."

Our Brazilian neighbors became fast friends of ours – they were mostly just happy that we were trying to learn. I'm sure if I had a tape recording of those first conversations, we would all chuckle at how basic our level of language understanding was, but that kind of raw conversation was exactly what we needed right then.

One day, the power went off and our neighbor had some electrical issues in his little apartment. He walked into our little apartment and asked "Gino" (my Portuguese name), can I plug an extension cord into your system so we can have electricity?" That was the very first gesture of trust and behavioral connection from our new Brazilian friend – reaching out to us for help.

This family had children the same age as ours and they would constantly play together. It was just so beautiful and heartwarming to see how the language barrier had no impact on our children while we struggled through those first stages of learning Portuguese. We became very close friends with these dear neighbors.

The Brazilian culture is very reflective and has such a colorful language: it's a dynamic world. We were told that if you want the best barbecue in the world, you'll find it in Brazil – and indeed we did. They have a restaurant that serves meat roasted on a spear over an open fire. They bring out a whole piece of beef roast or filet mignon, chicken, wild game, alligator, eel, an incredible array of different kinds of meats. Until you give them the signal that you're finished, they'll just keep bringing the meat out.

The place was called Chuhascaria, and we went there often. We went several times and enjoyed the simplicity of sitting out in the open night's very warm breeze. It was a special place for us that gave us many fond memories.

Approximately two weeks after we arrived in Brazil, the director of the Center received a message from the Bureau of Indian Affairs for Brazil. They had revoked the Summer Institute of Linguistics' authorization to work and live in the tribal locations of Brazil. Our organization, SIL/WBT, was being accused of mining Uranium dust and for security reasons they had blocked all foreigners' access to tribal locations.

Of course, this was a devastating jolt to our emotions. The Lord had so dramatically called us to Brazil, making it abundantly clear where and how we were going to be involved, and now we were having a door slammed in our faces right after we arrived in this place.

It felt like a death had occurred in the Center – the atmosphere was less lively than a funeral. The Wycliffe missionaries were grieving the loss of interacting and living with the tribal groups. These were people that had worked with and loved for years and several of the missionaries were nearing completion of translating the New Testament into that tribe's particular language. This was an extremely damaging blow to Wycliffe's progress.

Our family was faced with a terrifying decision: do we continue going to language school, or should we consider this a closed door and prepare to return to the U.S.? Was the Lord telling us this wasn't the time for us to be in Brazil? We spent a lot of time praying about this, searching for what God was telling us, and none of us had a sense that God had changed his mind. We were supposed to be in Brazil, so we continued with language school. This situation did add a level of excitement to language school for me, at least – not knowing how long we were going to be in the country heightened the level of urgency of our learning.

We completed the course and had become somewhat comfortable with the language; however, we still only had a very basic level of comprehension and our oral communication skills were rudimentary. I remember a good friend telling me that when you have your first dream in the language you're learning, that's when you know it's starting to become part of your thinking – part of your natural communication – and your learning will skyrocket from that point on.

And you know what? It happened just like my friend said it would.

I remember my first dream in Portuguese - I remember waking up and feeling so blissful, so happy. From that point on, learning the language became much easier.

We completed our training and prepared to fly to the interior of this country to a city named Porto Velho – the translation in English would be Old Port. It takes approximately 3 to 4 hours by jet to get from Belem, the city where we had just completed our language learning to this new one.

I remember getting off the jet and being greeted by a family that was happy for us to be there. The Wycliffe missionary that was the guest at that special church service in Denver the weekend a Cessna 206 plane was dedicated, was now greeting us at the airport, ready to give us a ride back to the Summer Institute of Linguistics Center, ten miles from the city of Proto Velho. Once we arrived there, we would begin the adventure of creating our new home and would begin our work as community development specialists.

Betty was a registered nurse, so she was there to work primarily with healthcare issues. I had business experience and, more importantly, knowledge of agriculture. My time growing up on a farm had given me some hands-on experience–and, of course, I still had that odd love for pigs.

We were able to rent a little house on the Center. No windows, just screens. Remember, now, it is unbearably, insufferably hot in the interior of Brazil. Nearly every day the temperature is between 95 and 120 degrees, and the humidity is in the low to mid 90's. During the rainy season the humidity is 100%. Naturally, we did everything imaginable to make sure that if there was even a chance for a breeze, there simply could not be anything blocking the few moments of cool air.

Even though we were in a completely new location, we still made an intentional effort to not just surround ourselves with the comfort zone of English-speaking missionaries. We sought to build relationships with new friends and make connections with the native Brazilians. By immersing ourselves in this new area, we managed to make some really good friends in the town, which was about ten miles from the Center.

Even though we had completed our schooling and switched locations, the tough times were far from over. This governmentally-enforced hiatus was especially difficult for the Wycliffe Bible Translators who had served in Brazil for years, unable to go back to their tribal home because the government had forbidden any contact with the various language groups in Brazil. We watched while they grieved, wanting so desperately to continue their translation work, to continue building relationships, and to minister to the people that God had called them to love.

They were emotionally, physically, and spiritually committed to providing the New Testament to language groups who'd never heard of the love of Jesus, of His promise to forgive our sins.

The Center director would make daily trips into town. Even though it was just a few miles, it would often take over an hour to get there because the road conditions were so poor.

After what seemed like an eternity of waiting around, the director called all of us missionaries to come to a meeting place.

He had news from a local government agent.

We were all equally parts excited and terrified.

As he began talking, it was quite clear that this was not going to be bad news. He was there to share an opportunity for my wife and I to visit a tribe, providing we would agree to have a government doctor come with us.

We were to travel to a tribe called the Deni because they were dying from yellow fever.

The local government representative was very much aware of Betty's credentials.

They kept close tabs on all foreigners within the country. Of course, they already had all of our information – we provided it to them in our application for the passports and visas. Since my Betty was a nurse, we were granted permission to go into this tribe. The Bureau of Indian Affairs was asking us to assist them in a mass effort to vaccinate all of the Deni people: adults, teenagers, babies.

This was going to be a huge task. The Deni tribe is not small, and they don't all live in the same village. We planned to spend as much time as necessary treating the sick and providing vaccinations for everyone.

One day, late in the afternoon, the chief walked over to me and indicated that he wanted to talk to me. In Portuguese as broken as my own, he shared with me that they had a need.

He said, "Gino, we have lost our last male hog. Would you be able to bring us a replacement?"

Can you imagine how happy I was to have a conversation with the chief? Here I am, talking to the chief leader of this group, the one who makes all of the decisions for his tribe. He was asking me to literally live out the dream I had while living in Denver, Colorado. I was flooded with joy in my spirit knowing that for this very reason, the Lord had given me a love for hogs so we could share God's love to a group of people who had never experienced the Love of Jesus.

With instant and incredible joy, I responded, "Yes. I would be *so happy* to return with a male hog."

VII
A Pig for the Deni

Betty and I had visited the Deni with the government doctor so that we could inject all of the Deni population for Yellow Fever. It was during this visit that the chief approached me about the possibility of bringing them back a male hog.

While I prepped to come back with this hog, I replayed that joyful conversation in my head again and again, savoring every sweet moment of that interaction. After multiple years, the Lord was showing us the reason He called us to serve the indigenous people in Brazil. Their need was my confirmation of our mission. The Deni's last male hog had died from a snake bite, so they didn't have the option of producing any more piglets. Getting this new hog was absolutely vital for the Deni's livelihood and prosperity – this was an incredibly important task I was taking on.

I was the only Wycliffe Bible Translator who *loved* hogs; everybody else thought they stank. While prepping to fly this hog in, I had to think about my family – after all, they were also in the "pigs stink" category of thought. Whether they stink or not, flying a hog around in a small aircraft is hardly a luxurious experience. So, in order to accommodate my family, I decided to build a box that would be just large enough to carry this male hog, without giving him any extra space to thrash around in.

Our Cessna 206 didn't need any extra turbulence. Flying in the jungle with only visual guidance did not allow any deviation from the most direct route possible. Then after arriving in the jungle location the landing demanded exact approach and touch-down…the plane had to be exactly lined up in order to land on a short strip that had been cleared from jungle trees and brush. Any movement by the plane could easily become tragic in a moment.

The flight lasts a little over three hours from Porto Velho to the Deni location, so I needed to have some kind of waterproof/drain-proof box. I constructed the main part of the box using heavy hardwood, then lined the bottom and sides with heavy tin so it would be as waterproof as possible.

I arranged the purchase of a male hog from a local Brazilian farmer who lived near the city of Porto Velho. I made sure he was in good health and even put it on a special grain diet to enhance the certainty of it surviving in the jungle.

Finally, the day came for me to book my flight to the Deni so I could deliver the hog.

This was an adventure I will surely never forget. This boy was incredibly unhappy with me – especially when it came to getting in his little box. Matter of fact, he fought several of us while we tried to put him into his tiny crate. We stuffed him in, latched the top so he couldn't escape, hurriedly loaded him into the back of the pickup, and off to the airport we went. We loaded our pig-headed miracle onto the plane, and Betty and I settled in for our three-hour flight to the Deni. The pilot went through his usual safety check, and pretty soon we were cleared for take-off.

This particular morning started out like one of those jungle days – one where the weather was absolutely beautiful - but by around 11 o'clock, the thunderclouds were rapidly rolling in.

We had misgauged our loading time and were not as far into the trip as we wanted to be by noontime. We now found ourselves flying into what looked like a very dark and sinister thunderstorm.

Flying in the jungle entailed flying without the luxury of radio contact with any tower, so we instead flew by VFR, or visual flight rules. We knew that if we entered that thundercloud, there was no way we would be able to see the ground, an incredibly serious decision to be made by the pilot. Instead, we would usually try to fly around it. That day's storm, however, was too big of a monster to evade. We just couldn't do it.

The pilot leaned over and said, "Dean, we're going to have to abort this flight. I'm just not willing to attempt to fly through this thunderstorm."

Reluctantly, I agreed with him, and back to the city of Porto Velho we went.

Several days later, we made a second attempt. This time, the weather was much more favorable and the flight was pretty smooth for jungle flying. At 5000 feet, the air is cool, and our hog friend was fairly relaxed for that part of the flight.

Then we started our descent for landing. I really thought I had built the crate small enough to keep the pig restrained, but he certainly found a lot of room in his little box to squirm around. He romped and fussed so much that it started to really affect the flight of our aircraft.

We were making our final approach to touchdown: one mile, now half a mile, all the while this hog is just thrashing up a storm. Our pilot had to make a quick decision. The jungle strips we landed on were not very wide or very long, and with our hog causing such a ruckus, our pilot was terribly concerned that if he didn't touch down at the perfect moment, our hog's fit could easily cause the plane to veer to either side of the airstrip, driving us into almost certain death.

Without talking to anyone, I could hear him on the radio proclaiming that we were aborting the landing. He quickly pulled our little Cessna into a steep climb to gain a safe altitude. While he circled the tribal location, I pleaded with the pilot to make another attempt.

With a reluctant grin on his face, he responded, "I'll try one more time, but can you please tell that hog to calm down!"

Luckily, our second landing attempt was much more successful. As we landed, the Deni Indians sprinted towards us in absolute excitement. Before we even got the engine shut off, they had surrounded us.

It was an absolute honor – a delight – to remove our special crate and open the lid of the hog's tiny prison. The Indians shrieked in utter joy.

Now, you may be wondering how we would control this hog without any fences or barn, no form of containment of any kind. You see, this particular tribe had never seen a corral or a barn. Hogs were their animals of choice because they would roam on their own but would eventually return to the village to get food. The Deni just made sure there was a constant supply of food and water for them and the pigs always found their way back to the tribe. We spent the rest of our day mingling with our "happy friends," and sharing pig stories.

Sure enough, a couple hours later, our hog returned to the airstrip to eat the food I had brought with me.

The pilot left the very next morning so he could return to Porto Velho. Our plan was to stay in this tribal location for about two months. We had to book what day he would re-trieve us from the Deni tribe to fly us back to the city before he could leave, and after we did so, he headed out and left us to do our work with our new Deni friends.

We immediately began working on several different projects the chief and I had decided we needed to accomplish. One of these projects was to teach this group basic math skills. In the interior of Brazil, the river traders send representa-tives into the area's different language groups to sell liquor or T-shirts or long pants – things the Indians valued. The mosquito population in the interior of Brazil is horrifyingly intense, so having a long-sleeved shirt or long pants makes life much more comfortable while working in the fields or cutting wood in the jungle.

These river traders would come in and sell these items at ridiculously inflated prices, knowing that the Indians would never be able to pay. In lieu of making a payment, they would demand that the Indians gather rubber from the rub-ber trees in the jungle and give it back to the river traders as bargaining chips. The traders would then bring the rubber to the cities and export it out of Brazil. It was heartbreak-ing to watch these innocent people being taken advantage of by these traders. It grieved me terribly to see them be-ing charged such outrageous amounts for simple T-shirts. They simply didn't have the math skills to understand what a T-shirt should really sell for, so they paid too much be-cause they desperately needed to have something to cover their mosquito-ridden bodies.

With this injustice in mind, I prepared what I thought would be a four-week basic math course. I scheduled class time in the morning, allowing time for the new learning to sink in before we met again in the evening to see if they could apply their newly learned math techniques. To my amazement, they gave me feedback with an intense accuracy. They repeated everything we had covered in class that day!

Part of me thought, *how could they do this? It takes us years to learn basic math skills, and yet this Indian tribal group was absorbing and applying these skills in a few short hours.*

One day, I came to a realization. If I had never had the opportunity to write a new thought on a piece of paper, the only way for me to recall it would be for me to burn it into my brain so I could keep it with me forever. This tribal group was extremely intelligent, and my four-week math course found itself completed in just over a week.

It was a thrill to see them learn, but it was also incredibly overwhelming to experience just how quickly they could hear a new concept, understand its principles, and then apply it within a matter of hours. Since we completed the course so quickly, we found ourselves with a lot of extra time. I spent hours and hours with the chief, working with him in the fields, visiting him in the evenings, and just trying my best to build a solid, long-term personal and professional relationship.

The night before our scheduled flight back to the city, the chief came up to our little house or, more accurately, a hut, since it was really just a four-pole structure with a thatched roof, maybe occupying a 10x10 living space. The chief came to our dwelling place and invited us to a Deni dance. We'd never been invited to anything like this, so we considered this invite a tremendous honor.

He said, "Gino, just bring something to eat and we'll be together tonight."

At least, that's what I *thought* he said.

So my wife fixed a nice dish of food, something we would consider very tasty and delicious: fresh pineapple we had found in the jungle, some other jungle fruits that were available to us, and some rice.

Having rice was not a staple food for the Indians since it wasn't grown in this area. If you had rice, it simply meant you were able to buy it either off of a river trader boat or bring it in from a nearby village or town. We thought that bringing rice as our dish for the dance would be a special treat for everyone.

This particular village is constructed in a sort of circular fashion. All of the houses are in a circle and they conduct all of their meetings in the center of this hub. For the dance, we eagerly walked our family into the circle, proudly carrying our little dish of food we brought to share with everyone.

We had understood the chief to say that this was going to be a potluck event, so we were looking forward to trying what everyone else had brought.

To us Americans, a potluck entails everyone bringing a dish to share together, but that is certainly not the definition of a Deni potluck. We soon realized that we had misunderstood the rules of the occasion.

All of the other families brought food for the dance. They all sat down inside the circle, but they immediately started eating their own food. They weren't sharing with anyone else.

But we had already begun to help ourselves to some of their food, doing what any American would do at a potluck. They kept laughing at us and we had absolutely no idea why. We simply couldn't figure out what was so funny to them.

It took us maybe 30 or 40 minutes before we realized that *no one else is taking food from other people's dishes.* Of course, we had been helping ourselves to their food this whole time. As best as I could, I apologized to them for the misunderstanding.

And they laughed and laughed and laughed and laughed.

They thought it was *so* funny.

We finished our meal and started a small fire in the middle of this little village, partly to keep the mosquitoes away and partly to give us just a little bit of light to see by. Nights in the jungle are extremely dark. We didn't have electricity, so the only light we had to cut into the darkness came from either a flashlight or a fire.

As the fire softly flickered, the chief walked over to Betty and me and handed us two beautiful headpieces. They were made out of very tightly woven bamboo fiber, and the head rings resembled frisbees. There were vibrant macaw feathers attached to the outside ring, and the backside had fiber string with tiny coconut seeds attached that were glued together with little macaw feathers.

The chief placed one of these exquisite pieces on my head, then Betty's, and in broken Portuguese proclaimed, "Let's dance!"

Here's this American couple dancing with the Deni Indians, moving to music you and I probably wouldn't really consider music. But to them it was, and we had ourselves a festive little soiree that dark night. They were so happy that we had been working with them, teaching them math skills, and especially for bringing them that hog.

The morning after the dance, we heard the glorious sound of a Cessna approaching. Although our visit to the Deni was a super success, we were ready to go home. This trip had been wonderful and fulfilling, but it was also incredibly stressful.

Our plane landed just fine, and we loaded our few possessions into the cargo bay, climbed in, and buckled our seatbelts. As I was getting settled, I noticed the chief coming up to me with a very serious look on his face.

He said, "Gino, because you came and brought us a male hog, we now know that you care for us, that you care for my people."

The pilot maneuvered a beautiful takeoff and we were quickly floating over the jungle. On our flight back to Porto Velho, I couldn't help but ponder the chief's statement.

> *Because we brought them a male hog,*
> *they knew that we cared?*

We had been there before to inject all of the Deni for Yellow Fever – which saved the lives of many – and yet they didn't comprehend, they didn't realize, that we were showing them care and love? But when we were able to deliver them a pig, NOW they knew we cared for them?

––––––

Remember how God called us into Wycliffe? It all started with them needing someone who loved pigs, and someone who wanted to work with Indians. God tasked us with the holy assignment to work and live in Brazil, and our visit to the Deni wholly affirmed that calling. Pigs and Indians, that's all it took.

If you find yourself questioning God's calling today – you're not sure exactly what you're supposed to do, or you're unsure what His call is really about – I want to encourage you to do a very quick internal review of yourself. What is it that you just *love* to do? How do you love to serve? How do you want to demonstrate God's love to others?

I wholeheartedly believe that the answers to those questions will reveal God's call on your life.

Psalm 139: 1-13 says, *"You have searched me Lord and you know me. You know when I sit and when I rise: you perceive my inner thoughts...for you created my inmost being; you knit me together in my mother's womb.*

―――――

You are created to be exactly the person that you are today. His word clearly tells us to be faithful to what He's given us, and may I encourage you, no matter how strange or how different you may be from others around you, the Lord created you exactly as you are. You are the person He wants to show His love to those who have not yet experienced it.

You are exactly who you need to be.

You are enough.

Embrace your own weirdness and experience the amazing journey God has planned for you. After all, my family's journey started with an obsession with pigs and Indians.

VIII
Clearing the Deni Airstrip

Several months had passed since we'd delivered the hog to the Deni, and I had scheduled a follow-up visit to see how successful our efforts had been. Not only did we want to check in on the hog we'd brought in, but we wanted to see how much of my math courses had stuck with them.

No one had travelled to this location for several months, and the airstrip hadn't been maintained in our absence, so it was impossible to fly in. This meant we needed to explore alternative transportation options. We used a vehicle as far as the roads would possibly allow out of Porto Velho, then we got tickets to take a riverboat as far into the interior as we could. After exhausting those methods, we hired a native Brazilian who had a canoe with a motor so that he could take us the rest of the way into the Deni's location in the jungle.

It took us 3 ½ days to get back to the Deni. Of course, if we had been able to fly, it would have taken us about three hours. The value of having access to an aircraft in the jungle was never lost on us missionaries – it was an invaluable resource. We were incredibly blessed to work with some amazing organizations who provided this wonderful tool for us: Jungle Aviation Fellowship (JAF), Missionary Aviation Fellowship (MAF), and Jungle Aviation and Radio Service (JAARS).

We arrived at the Deni location to find that the little house – well, hut – we'd previously lived in had already fallen down from a termite infestation. Jungle houses don't last very long. The wood that's used to hold up the roof is very green and terribly soft. The thatched roofs rot and deteriorate quickly, so these shelters have a very short lifespan.

We had no choice but to start completely over and build ourselves another shelter. Luckily, we had received all of that training in jungle camp, so this task wasn't too difficult – just lots and lots of very hard labor. We built our little shelter and had something to protect us from at least a little bit of the rain.

Next on our list was that airstrip. We worked directly with the Chief, and I went through the process of hiring Indians to help us clear the jungle overgrowth that had sprouted since the last time it had been cut. We didn't have the luxury of lawnmowers, so we were entirely dependent upon manpower and machetes to get that airstrip cleared.

It took us several hot and sweaty hours to cut the required 10,000 feet for the landing strip. Plus, we had to manicure an approach on each end, adding an additional 5,000 feet of work.

I also brought along a second level of math training curriculum with us, so we would clear the airstrip in the morning until it got so hot we just couldn't stand it any longer, and then we'd sit under the shade and work on math. When it would finally cool off enough for us to work again, we would go back out and cut on the airstrip until the night's darkness covered the jungle.

It was necessary for us to get the airstrip cleared because there were translators who had been on furlough in Canada who were soon coming to work with the Deni. Making the village accessible by air meant they wouldn't have the same long and arduous journey we had just endured.

While we were out working, I always tried to use the time to learn and understand more of the Deni culture. They loved it when I would try to talk to them in Deni instead of Portuguese, and I like to think the hard work lessened the brokenness of my developing Deni.

One day, we found ourselves deeply in need of a rest. I had hired about ten men to cut with me, and we had probably cleared around 50 feet of the airstrip already. It had gotten hot – unbelievably hot. I didn't have a thermometer with me, but I suspect it was probably around 120 degrees at seven o'clock that morning. Due to the incredible heat that day, we decided to take a break from our math class, similar to taking a snow day in the U.S.

Around noontime, we decided to walk down to the river as a family just so we could get in the water as a reprieve from the sweltering heat. It took quite a while to actually make it to the river on this path since we had to walk single file on the new trail that had been cleared. Betty and I had taken our children with us this time, and our daughter was in line right behind me.

As kids do, she tripped on something and fell – right flat on her face.

Naturally, we immediately stopped to see what happened and what I saw was absolutely horrifying.

Her eyeball was *bleeding*.

My mind started to race at the sight of her little face. She must have fell on something – a rock, maybe? But I didn't see one and I had no idea what had caused this catastrophe.

Then I saw it – this sharp needle –the end of a twig standing ramrod straight smack in the middle of the path.

When they'd cleared the path with a machete, they had cut this tree seedling.

Unfortunately, it had left a pointed spike perfectly made for gouging my daughter's eyeball. We raced her back to our little house so that we could try to relieve her pain somehow. We tried to rinse it with water so we could clean the mud out of her eye, but our sweet, little girl just kept crying and crying and crying. The Indians became very concerned and our daughter's injury became somewhat of a spectacle as they kept coming to check on her and see what had happened.

All I had to say was that she must have stabbed her eye on a twig sized spear in the middle of the path.

There wasn't a hospital for us to take her to, no emergency room to race into, no ambulance staffed with paramedics to come assuage our fears. We didn't even have a radio to call for help or to beg for a plane to come back earlier for us. Even if we could have gotten a plane in early, the airstrip was still a death trap – there was no way a plane was getting in there.

Our only option was to seek God's grace and pray.

Father, have mercy. Have mercy on this sweet little baby's eye, have mercy on the damage that may have been done to it already. Lord, please give us comfort, give her comfort. Please heal our little girl.

It was a long afternoon and evening for our family as we sat and prayed.

The Deni were watching us, inquisitive about what we were doing in this time of crisis. They didn't know Jesus yet, but they had some questions.

"Who are you talking to?" they would ask while we prayed.

This terrifying ordeal turned into a moment of demonstration for the Deni. It gave us an amazing opportunity to show our honest, raw faith as we turned to the Almighty God, Jehovah-Jireh, as our provider and our healer.

This seemed very strange to them.

When I woke the next morning, I found myself anxiously anticipating what God had done through the night. It was a long night of unrest for us, but, amazingly, our little daughter slept quite well.

I was eager to see if the Lord was healing our little girl – I believed with all of my being that He could.

The bleeding had stopped, but the swelling was still quite intense. We knew that God's healing touch was upon her and that she was going to be okay.

What we didn't know, however, was whether this would have any sort of long-term effect on her vision.

Our afternoon plan to escape the heat turned into a test of our faith.

Fast forward to today, and this little girl is now a mother to beautiful children of her own and she has no issues whatsoever with her eye. She does have a little dot on her eyeball – a constant reminder of our Lord's healing power. When I look at her face and see this "prayer marker," it just reminds me of how Almighty our God really is.

––––––

Perhaps you feel like you're in a jungle today. Maybe it isn't a literal jungle, but you feel like the only hope of help you have is coming from God – just like we had on that dreary day. Maybe you have an experience of crisis in your own life that has left a scar, a mark, for you to remember this trauma. Let that memory, that mark, turn into an expression of worship. Relish in the demonstrated proof that God provided help at the very moment you needed His touch.

October 8, 2007

II Cor. 9:10-13

Now may He who supplies seed to the sower, and bread for food, supply and multiply the seed you have sown and increase the fruits of your righteousness, while you are enriched in everything for all liberality, which causes thanksgiving through us to God. For the administration of this service not only supplies the needs of the saints, but also is abounding through many thanksgivings to God, while

through the proof of this ministry, they glorify God for the
obedience of your confession to the gospel of Christ, and
for your liberal sharing with them and all men.

In 1971, my wife Betty and I moved from Southern California to the Denver area when we became aware of a church situation that Pastor Blair and his family were going through a very difficult time in their lives. Not only was the community turning against them, as a family they were also suffering as tremendous financial pressures were mounting, causing some intense pain and stress. I had grown up in a Christian environment, but never understood the power of "giving," but the Lord in His great mercy allowed me to meet my wife Betty, who has a powerful gift of giving. Together we decided to begin to give food to this Pastor and his family, as a test to see how the Lord would bless our commitment.

Almost immediately, He provided us with unique food supplies out of the ordinary. Packs of frozen meat would be laying on the street in front of my car, companies returning rental trailers for a company that was employing me, would turn in their rentals, only to realize that they had failed to deliver all of the food supplies in the trailer and asked me to dispose of it for them, etc. Then one day the passage from II Cor. 9:10-13 became a passion of ours and we decided to plant a garden and promised the Lord that we would give half of the harvest to Pastor Blair and his family.

This pilot garden was not located in the most fertile ground in Colorado, but rather up in the windswept area of Parker.

The Lord honored our commitment and while the actual garden plants were weather beaten, the amount of vegetables produced was tremendous. We literally filled our pantry, all the while giving half to the Blair family. It was difficult for me to walk up to this super successful Pastor and his wife, carrying a box of the Lord's provision, but at the same time, feeling the intense power in the gift of giving. A number of times I would drive up to the church (Calvary Temple) in our VW van and have a conversation with myself – *What are you doing? This Pastor doesn't need my box of vegetables, and frozen meat packages.* Little did we realize that behind the scenes, Pastor and Betty Blair, were not only receiving our gift, but also providing food to their family. The Lord was beginning a food ministry for us that continues to this day.

This model of giving developed deeper and deeper into our spirit and within a couple of years, the Lord called us to work with Wycliffe Bible translators focusing our efforts with various tribal groups living in the interior of Brazil. The major areas of activity we were asked to conduct was teaching basic health care and developing food supplies for those special language groups that were suffering from poor health and inconsistent food sources. The ripple effect from our "giving class" while living in the Denver area was now continuing. Now rather than helping one family, we were asked to make an impact in the lives of five different language groups. Again, the Lord honored these efforts as we introduced appropriate food sources, such as rice, corn, etc. We had the opportunity to provide food for the hungry people living in the interior jungle of Brazil. While Betty was treating the sick, and teaching them how to administer basic medicines, I was operating on the same principle with training models of food production.

After working 23 years with Wycliffe, the Lord changed our assignment location back to California, where we opened a non-profit ministry, Springboard Ministry Inc., a counseling center (Center of Attention) dedicated to provide mental health services to the underserved and homeless population. After just a short time, it became very clear to us that people were hungry, both spiritually as well as physically and so the ripple effect continued as we linked together with a Vietnamese family dedicated to prepare at least one hot meal each week.

Now ten years later, we were feeding approximately 500-600 homeless a hot meal each month. The Lord continues to provide this food from unique sources, such as Pizza Hut, KFC, and the local food bank. During the last year we served over 5,000 lbs. of food to hungry souls living on the streets of Santa Ana California.

The Lord blessed Springboard ministry, and while we are feeding the homeless, He has also allowed us the privilege of providing food to four families who are living in the area. Many of them are having a very difficult time putting food on their table.

For the administration of this service not only supplies the needs of the saints, but also is abounding through many thanksgivings to God, while through the proof of this ministry, they glorify God for the obedience of your confession to the gospel of Christ, and for your liberal sharing with them and all men. II Corinthians 9:12

The ripple affect continues and only the Lord knows the contents of our next chapter yet to be written!

Dean Kroeker

───────

While we were living in Castle Rock, we enjoyed watching Pastor Blair on TV Sunday mornings. One Sunday we heard him say they had a fire in their home and we knew there were financial difficulties as well. I wondered if they might like some of the canning that we had put up from our garden. Dean took a case of green beans to the church the next week and they were welcomed. Eventually we moved into Denver and started attending Calvary Temple and the case of green beans turned into weekly trips of whatever the Lord supplied that week. Frozen meat off of rental trucks left right in front of us. I would walk down the street and someone would come out of their house and ask me if I wanted to pick the apples from their tree. We were living in the realm of the Lord's blessings on a daily basis.

It was in the midst of that sharing what the Lord provided for the Blair's and us that the Lord called us into missions. Little did we know that sharing food would follow us as a part of what the Lord had for us throughout the years. Regardless of what our job descriptions were, it seemed that a food ministry ended up being a part of what we did. In Brazil we were assigned as Community Development Specialists and our work was teaching indigenous people how to grow food crops and upgrade their nutrition. In Huntington Beach, Dean was in charge of the food bank for Wycliffe missionaries. In Santa Ana, we fed and shared the gospel with approximately 10,000 homeless people each year on the streets of Santa Ana, California.

Through these experiences the Lord taught us how to freely give, trust in Him, and exercise our faith. When we were in the jungles of Brazil, there were times when our food would run out and because of the preparation the Lord had given us, it was with ease that we could trust Him to feed us during what normally would have been times of deep stress.

There was a time when the Lord was teaching us how to be doers and not hearers of the Word only, and we even went on trips into the jungle without food because of the Scriptures where the Lord instructed the disciples to not take provisions with them. I can still taste the food He provided during those trips and remember the greater openness to the gospel on those particular tribal visits. Our preparation for this walk started with a case of green beans. It was as if we had our own personalized Bible school at Calvary Temple, while feeding the Blair's. Looking back, it is easy to see how He has fulfilled the passage. "No eye has seen, no ear has heard, no mind can conceive what God has prepared for those who love him."

Betty Kroeker

I. First Sewing Student

II. River Trader Boat

III. Road to Puerto Velho

IV. Porto Velho Airport

V. Food Provisions

VI. Labrea

VII. Rescue from Jungle Camp

VIII. Jungle Camp Rescue Plane

IX. Classroom at Jungle Camp

X. House in Piraha

XI. Home School

XII. Help is on the Way!

XIII. My Gracious Wife, Betty

XIV. Dying Native Baby

XV. Clearing the Airstrip

XVI. Clearing the Airstrip

XVII. First Corn Planting

XVIII. First Jungle Boards

Psalm 91:4

He will cover you with his feathers.
He will shelter you with his wings.
His faithful promises are your armor and protection.

IX
Jungle Flights

In the United States, we're kind of accustomed to a particular routine when it comes to flying: get your boarding pass; check your luggage or lug your carry-on around with you; find your gate and check in; traipse onto the aircraft and find your designated seat; then wait for the complimentary snack and quietly hope there isn't much turbulence on your trip.

Flying in the jungle is nothing like that.

Every pound/kilo has to be weighed to ensure a safe flight. Not only do the passengers have to weigh in each time they fly, but they also have to weigh every food item, all supplies, and any medicine being brought along. Literally everything we wanted to take with us on the flight had to be weighed.

Flying over the jungle is an amazing experience. From above, all of the trees look like a carpet of green foliage. They're beautiful trees with flowers, and, at the right season, many of those flowers are this deep lavender color. Every once in a while, you get lucky and come across macaws flying in pairs over the jungle with you. Their colorful magnificence coupled with the sheer beauty of the jungle is a truly breathtaking experience.

I vividly remember one of our flights in particular. We were flying to a tribal location, and I was sitting in the seat next to the pilot, watching and observing him while he kept a close eye on the instruments and clouds as we soared over the jungle. I was relishing in the joy of staring down at the jungle, admiring God's creation, when I noticed out of the corner of my eye that some of the gauges on the instrument panel weren't functioning properly. As a passenger, it's terribly concerning to see the fuel gauge showing near empty when you know that there's still at least two hours of flying left before you can land. Looking at that fuel gauge was giving me an otherworldly amount of stress.

I was wearing a headset – as we usually did – and I knew I wasn't going to be able to keep quiet while I anxiously awaited our certain doom. With the worry about a fiery crash in my voice, I piped up, "Uh, I can't help but notice that we're nearly out of fuel and I know there's absolutely nowhere for us to land out here. Do you have some sort of plan for this or are we just going to die out here?"

The only sane way to take a plane from an airport into a jungle location is to have a prepared airstrip waiting for you to land on, and those airstrips take days – weeks, even – to clear. My stress about the fuel situation was well-founded.

The pilot looked at me and laughed, "Dean, just relax. That fuel gauge hasn't worked for the last two years."

You know, for somebody that isn't a pilot and doesn't have any experience maintaining airplanes, this was hardly a relaxing response. He then went on to inform me that all good pilots fly by time, not by watching gauges. He knew exactly how much fuel we had in that plane, and that we had enough to land at the jungle location and return to the city.

I decided it was time to stop looking at the gauges and go back to looking at the scenery.

Each of our family members had a different response to jungle flying. My wife, Betty, would frequently have to take airsickness medicine before the flight because her stomach had a very high tendency to get upset during our flights. So about two or three hours before the flight she would take this medicine which gave her all kinds of other ailments: severe headaches, dizziness, and all kinds of other unsavory side effects.

At least it was better than getting sick in-flight or immediately after landing.

Many of our flights required at least two hours, and we occasionally visited a location that was just over three hours one way. Usually her airsickness medicine would work – to some extent – for the duration of the flight, but sometimes it would have already worn off by the time we landed. Needless to say, Betty never really enjoyed our jungle flights.

One of our sons just decided that the best mode of operation when you're going to fly in the jungle is to just go to sleep. Before the plane even left the ground, that little guy was sitting there in his seat fast asleep.

Another son would always hope that it would be a rough ride. He would often say, "Dad, I hope this is a bumpy flight." To him, the rougher the flight, the more exciting of an adventure it was.

Our daughter would endure the flight by constantly singing. Before we would even take off, she'd start singing – making up songs, making up words. Her songs didn't necessarily have any meaning, but she just needed to sing.

Flying with the Kroekers in tow was always a menagerie of emotions.

When you fly through the rainforest, you frequently encounter thunderclouds. On this occasion the pilot had determined that we were going to attempt to fly through this dark thunder cloud. I liked to look in awe at those great big, powerful thunderbolts. I usually caught myself thinking, "Well, this one is going to be bumpy."

Usually when you fly into these clouds, the initial entrance into the cloud causes a significant jolt, but flying inside of it is pretty smooth. Then, when you finally reach the edge of the thundercloud, it kind of kicks you out and propels you forward with another strong jolt.

One of the biggest components of flying in the jungle actually has nothing to do with the actual flight itself: the landing strip. For the flights we're used to in America, landing is just another natural part of the easy process. In the jungle, however, it takes a lot of planning and preparation to land a plane safely.

I specifically remember one of the strips we encountered in Brazil. It was built by the Indians and the translation team, and it was located in a place where there were not long stretches of level ground. In order to make due, the jungle approach had been cut for the airstrip with the very last 50 to 75 yards at a rather steep incline – probably around 20° – at the end of this airstrip. It was actually very relieving to know that when you're landing and touching down on the grass that you're going have this incline at the end to help slow the plane down and bring it to a stop. On the other hand, when you're taking off from the highest part of the strip you're looking down a 20° slope. It appears, and feels like, you're driving right down into the dirt.

Of course, the skilled jungle pilots have maneuvered this takeoff many times and they know exactly how to pick up enough speed to get just enough lift to clear the trees. It was always a relief to finally feel those wheels leaving the earth and realize you'd survived one more successful takeoff.

One of the tribes that we worked with was located in an area where it was impossible to build an airstrip, primarily because the land, which was a potential location to cut an airstrip, simply wasn't level enough for the required distance to land a Cessna 206. Instead, we actually had to hire a seaplane that would be able to land either on the river, or on a rather large lake near the location where we were working.

It was a wonderful blessing for us to have access to a seaplane but flying onto the water meant we had to hike at least eight hours to get into the village. On one of our trips to this location it was my intent to teach the Indians how to construct a house out of lumber. Up to this point, they would build their houses simply out of jungle material and, depending on the time and the resources available to them, they would literally cut the trees that were closest to the location where they wanted to live, thus making it easier to construct.

However, this mode of construction made these houses very temporary. The jungle termites would literally destroy a house in less than a year. I wanted to create a model for them that would show them how to build a house that wasn't temporary. I needed to use boards and lumber cut from hardwood trees so that the lifetime of their houses would surpass that of their simple stick house with thatched roofs and split palm floors.

Flying lumber into a jungle location proved to be very difficult. This particular seaplane that we were using had just enough space under the cabin area that I could attach a 4' x 8' sheet of plywood to make the flight. On this particular trip, the pilot expressed great concern and stress: having a sheet of plywood underneath the cabin could change the dynamics required for this plane to be airborne. Even though we had secured it to the best of our ability, some of the rope that we used to secure the wood started to loosen during the flight. Although the movement was slight, it was certainly enough to compete with the pilot's ability to fly the plane.

When we finally landed on the water, I remember all of us letting out a huge shout. "Praise God! We made it safely!"

We made this same flight several more times before we were finally able to gather enough wood to begin the construction.

Living in the jungle meant we would be living in a remote location, but it also meant we had no access to communication with the outside world: the mission organization didn't have a license to operate radios. Before we could fly out to a jungle location, we made arrangements for the plane to return and take us back to the Center in Porto Velho.

Every time we flew in – whether we took a boat or any other kind of transportation – I would ask the pilot back at the Center to please give us a mail drop if they were flying over our location en route to another language group, either flying translators in or out of their tribal locations.

There was one location that we went to that was especially difficult: the Paumari. We were there for a number of weeks and we had no choice but to leave our children back at the Center so they could continue with their schooling.

It was an incredibly difficult living situation for us.

We were blessed back at the Center to have what we refer to as *children's home parents*: missionary couples that were in the country specifically to take care of the children of other missionaries while they were in the tribal locations.

Under these circumstances, having a chance to get mail – or even tape recordings – that connected us to our family was inexpressibly special. I remember one of these visits where Betty and I found ourselves feeling especially isolated. We missed our kids, we missed getting letters from our friends in the states, and we missed the letters from the churches that were supporting us. We were lonely.

On a very hot, muggy morning, I heard the glorious sound of a Cessna 206 approaching. In the jungle, sound travels for a really long distance because there's really nothing out there to interfere with it. There's no loud music being played, no traffic.

The jungle is surprisingly quiet.

Every once in a while, you might hear some monkeys chattering, or maybe some jaguars growling, but most days it stayed pretty silent.

When I heard this plane, my spirits were instantly lifted. We had talked to the pilot about dropping mail for us if he was ever flying over our village, and I was desperately hoping he was there to bring us a little piece of home. As he was approaching and we could finally see him through the little clearing in the jungle, I remember thinking, *he is really high.*

We saw him give us the signal, slightly tipping his wings to indicate he was preparing to give us a mail drop. But he was so high that I was really concerned that he wouldn't be able to drop the package at just the right moment so it would land in the little clearing around our village. At this point, many of the Indians had gathered around in excitement, too. We had done this a few times previously, so they knew what was about to happen.

The plane was circling our little village: I could barely see him open his window and drop out a little package.

But something went wrong. Terribly wrong.

It must have caught on the side of the window or something sharp and the package ripped wide open just as he was letting go.

All we could see was this rain of envelopes floating down into the jungle.

It's very rare for there to be any kind of wind or air movement in the jungle, but on this day, there was a slight breeze. The envelopes sprinkled down to the ground. A few of them did land in our clearing, but most of the mail just dropped into the abyss of the forest.

Our feeble joy was shattered instantly.

I was so sad. Betty and I were so desperate to hear from our children and now we would have to scrounge through the jungle just to have a chance of finding what they had sent us.

The Indians sprinted into the jungle to look for anything they could find and we did manage to obtain a few letters. We found one from our kids – and it was wonderful – but it was still so sad knowing there was a lot of mail that we would never even see.

Days later, the Indians were still finding remnants of the drop. They found pieces of paper and an envelope or two, half of which was already eaten by termites and ants. We never really knew most of what was in the package.

Though horribly painful, this experience reminded us again that the Lord is in control. The phrase, *I will trust in You* became very special to us.

He will cover us with his feathers and
under his wings I will find refuge.
His faithfulness will be my shield and my protection.

X

A Legend from Paumari

When I got to Brazil and started working with the tribal groups, I started to learn a lot about the land: the culture, geography, nature, the folklore. I learned that there were pink dolphins swimming in the rivers, which was something I had never heard of before. I had no idea dolphins even lived in freshwater.

They were incredible. You would be going up and down the rivers in the middle of the Amazon rainforest and there would be pink dolphins swimming right alongside you. They were huge. They would come right up to the side of your canoe, and it was like they were reaching out, trying to talk to you. Finally, I had to ask the chief about this phenomenon.

He was really anxious to tell me about them. "Gino, we believe that the dolphins come and rescue us if someone has an accident or drowns. They come and pick up our souls and take them to the bottom of the sea so our souls can live eternally."

Immediately, I knew I had a relevant avenue to explain Christ's loving forgiveness. We don't put our faith in a dolphin to carry us into eternal glory – that's why Jesus died for us.

From that day on, I made sure to connect our worship services to the legend of the pink dolphin: Christ, our Redeemer, has come to save us. At that point, there weren't any believers in the Paumari, but we were sowing seeds. We were trusting in the Lord's perfect timing to call our friends to Him.

Living with the Paumari started to feel like living in a graveyard. We buried a lot of babies, adults, kids – too many. They were dying from drinking nasty, unsanitary water, and from the mosquitoes. Malaria is rampant in these parts of the world.

Right before sunset every night, you could hear the mosquitoes roar into the village, pillaging the area as fast as their wings could take them. If you weren't completely covered, you were in trouble. The Paumari had limited clothing, and they were desperate to get more so they could protect themselves from the mosquitoes. Every time we would go back to their village we would bring as much clothing as we could carry: shirts, pants, shorts, anything to cover their bodies.

We would often make trips back to the Center to get supplies, or to take care of research needs that we had encountered that were directly linked to the agricultural efforts I was planning or Betty need to make certain we had the best medicines with us to treat the issues the tribe was facing at that time, or any health issues. Just as we were prepping to head back from one of those trips, we got the idea to take a sewing machine with us. We thought it would be great to take some really simple clothing patterns and teach some of the Indians how to use the machine. It wasn't feasible to teach all of the Indians, of course, so we decided our plan would be to teach some of them, but only if they agreed to teach someone else in return – kind of like Romans 2:21 *you, therefore, who teach another, do you not teach yourself?*

We were excited about what this could mean for this tribe: we were hoping to start a domino effect in their community that would vastly improve their day to day living. I was especially excited about this effort because it meant I could implement a simple gesture that I learned while attending sales training during my time working with Fruehauf Trailer Corporations in Denver, Colorado. My family and I had personally committed to working ourselves out of a job from the very first day we arrived at the village. This was a practice I had started while working in sales, and I was eager to try it out in the jungle with the Paumari.

I went to a local hardware store in the little city of Porto Velho and was shocked by what I found: a Singer treadle sewing machine. Here in the U.S., you're lucky to find one of those in an antique store or maybe the farm sale of someone who is quite elderly. But in Porto Velho? They're selling them new and they're selling them cheap. We bought one and went to the fabric store to buy some material to sew with. We ended up with a bolt of cotton fabric with a simple pattern, a yellowish orange color that wouldn't show dirt right away. Then we picked up a couple of patterns for the ladies – A-lines, I think. We wanted to get them something simple so they could cut material and have nearly instant success.

We loaded up all of our materials – medicine, t-shirts, pants, shorts, blankets, and anything else we needed – and hired a JAARS airplane to fly us as far as we could possibly go via air travel. We landed in a little village out of the jungle called Labrea, and from there we had to hire a boat to take us upriver. There were trader boats that traveled up and down the river to trade goods for whatever was in season: rubber, hides, or whatever the nationals were harvesting at that particular time. Hiring one of these boats wasn't an easy venture – it's not like hiring a private boat. You are on their schedule. They would eventually get you to where you needed to go, but it usually took a few days.

And take a few days this trip certainly did.

Traveling on the river for three days when the distance is

covered by a 45-minute flight is utterly exhausting. It isn't too bad while you're moving on the river where there's a cool breeze, but the second the boat stops and pulls up the bank to tie up, the mosquitoes completely engulf you. On top of that, it was stiflingly hot without the breeze. The humidity was around 100% every single day and night, so we were always grateful to see the captain of the boat come back in and ask the guy down in the engine room to "start 'er up again."

Finally, we got to our location.

I had sent in a message to the Paumari chief to let him know we were coming back. I asked him to meet us at the riverbank with three or four canoes so we could haul everything back to the village. Even during rainy season, it was quite a trek to get back to our jungle home.

The Indians eagerly watched us unpack our stuff; they wanted to see what we checked off of their wish list. They always wanted to know if I brought gunpowder, fishhooks, sardines – things we take for granted back home. As we unloaded the sewing machine, the Paumari kept asking, "What is this? What is it?"

"I'll explain once we get to our house."

It was fun to watch them. Their culture has such a different way of processing newness than we Americans do. When we go to the grocery store to buy bread, we pinch it to see if it's fresh. The Paumari smell it. So, there they were, smelling this new piece of machinery their brains were trying to comprehend. They were utterly fascinated by this strange contraption – they'd never seen anything like it.

Amidst the throngs of curious Indians was a newlywed couple in their little canoe. In American culture, we give rings, but in this culture the new husband makes his wife a canoe instead. The young man eagerly volunteered to take the new sewing machine back to the house in his little tippy canoe. I felt like I needed to trust this young man, but it was really difficult -- those canoes are just so tippy. I could feel the Holy Spirit tugging on my heart to give him the opportunity to be the captain of my sewing machine's fate, but it was hard to trust that unsteady little canoe.

But I listened to the Holy Spirit and let fate run its course.

The Paumari were a joyous bunch. They talked and laughed together for the whole trip, which was nice because it gave me a chance to learn some new words and pick up some new terms while I observed Paumari comedy. It took about eight hours after disembarking from the river trader's boat, but we finally got home. They were happy to help carry stuff into our house – all the while carrying our kids along with their own.

They had become our dear friends.

This partially stemmed from the chief, Fari, and I cultivating a deep friendship. Betty and I were starting to really enjoy the comradery of this group – even the company of the young adults. Our Paumari friends carried all our things: medicines, clothing, food, everything we brought with us. We tried to limit what we brought with us to locations like this because we really wanted to try and live more like the locals. As they carried the sewing machine up to the house, they kept asking, "What is this?"

I repeated what I'd already said at least 15 or 20 times, "We will show you how to use it if you promise to teach someone else. We will teach you right out of Romans 8."

I am fully convinced, my dear brothers and sisters, that you are full of goodness. You know these things so well so you can teach others all about them.

My wife had made pre-cut A-line patterns before we left for the village. She opened up her little suitcase, took out the material, and, in just a few minutes, had sewn up a little dress. We were already familiar with Paumari culture, so we knew that the men must be the first ones to learn new skills – they were the ones we needed to win over in order to make this project work.

Luckily, Paumari fathers love their daughters as much as American daddies do. We were strategic: Betty's first project was to sew up a little dress for the chief's daughter.

The Paumari were fascinated with what Betty was doing. They hovered around us – anxiously waiting in anticipation in the sweltering jungle heat. We gathered in this ramshackle grass hut of a house, a breeze nowhere to be found, our hot bodies mushed together in a soup of body odor and sweat.

As Betty started to sew, I could see them trying to decipher what on earth was happening:

Oh my goodness! What is she doing? What is this machine doing? Why is this fish hook going up and down so rapidly?

They were completely flabbergasted by this sewing business. Betty finished stitching the dress, turned it right side out, and handed it to the chief's daughter.

You should've seen her face. She immediately slipped into the little dress, her eyes twinkling with the purest of joy. This was the first dress she'd ever worn. The chief was ecstatic to know that his daughter wasn't going to be devoured by mosquitoes that night. As soon as she put the dress on, the sweaty crowd erupted, "Make me one! Make me one!"

I reminded them of what I'd already repeatedly said at the riverbank and all the way canoeing to our jungle house: we will teach you if you promise to teach someone else. In my best rendition of their language, I asked, "Who is willing to teach someone else if we teach you how to use this sewing machine?"

What was once a house full of boisterous joy and excitement quickly fizzled into uneasy silence. Some of the families just hung their heads and dejectedly walked away. Fari, the chief, gave me an intense stare. "Gino, teach me how to use the machine."

"Fari, I would love to. Are you willing to teach someone else?"

With a sad look, he got up and left the house.

Our brilliantly crafted plan was deteriorating right before our eyes. Within just a few hours, our dreams had been crushed. My sales methods didn't work in the jungle like they did in America. The next few days and weeks were brutal for us. The relationships that we had worked so hard to build were untangling.

It was all falling apart.

Several nights later, the chief's little daughter approached Betty in private. "I'm willing to teach someone else how to make a dress if you teach me."

We finally had a volunteer.

Never in our right minds would we have planned to start our process by teaching a young girl. Not only were we violating the Paumari culture by not teaching the men first, but we were also doing so by teaching one of the lowest members of their society. Even in eating meals, the small girls were the last to get food. They were only fed if there was food leftover after the men and boys had eaten.

On top of that, she was the chief's daughter, and teaching her would disregard their cultural boundaries...but we had made a commitment to teach anyone willing to teach someone else.

We invited her up to our little house, opened up the sewing machine, and unfolded enough of the cotton material to make her a little dress. We started to teach her how to use the scissors and then we let her actually start sewing her dress.

It was probably the single ugliest sewing job I've ever seen in my life. But it didn't matter. Our dream was becoming reality through this little girl.

She finished her dress and took it back to her little hut, only to return a few minutes later with her mother in tow.

Not only had we breached Paumari culture by teaching a lowly little girl first, but now we were desecrating it even further by teaching none other than the chief's wife. The Lord was really testing our commitment.

The girl's mother was a quick learner – she had natural seamstress skills. With her little girl at her side, she started to make clothes for her family. I'll never forget, about a year after this moment we were leaving that tribe after one of our visits. They had become skilled seamstresses at that point – we were even able to obtain several more machines and they were now adeptly making clothes for the whole region.

It was incredible to witness this transformation – it always reminds me of the passage in Luke 12:

...to whom much is given, much is required...

We had committed ourselves to teaching the Paumari and it was incredible to see them making the same commitment to each other.

XI
Paumari

After several trips to the Paumari, we had started to build meaningful relationships with the leaders of the tribe and their families. Wycliffe was looking for someone to serve as a male influence in the New Testament translation process, and they asked my family if we'd consider working with the Paumari for several years. The translators already assigned to the tribe were two ladies serving as linguists who were diligently working on translating the New Testament. However, being female put them at a severe cultural disadvantage, which is why Wycliffe was looking for a male influence.

Wycliffe and the Summer Institute of Linguistics asked us to go in as a family so that we could build relationships with the men. We needed to gain their trust so that we could understand their perspective. We needed to incorporate the male view of Paumari traditions and history into the New

Testament translation – men even used verbs and nouns differently than the women did in conversation.

I had already become very close friends with Fari, the chief. Betty and his wife had also really hit it off and our children played together every day for hours. We had found wonderful friends there in the middle of the Amazon basin. After we had returned from our furloughs to the U.S., Wycliffe Bible Translators assigned us to work full-time with the Paumari.

We couldn't have been more excited.

Just like how people don't all live in the same city in the U.S., the Paumari don't all live in the same location. Before we started our assignment, we needed to decide which of the three main Paumari locations we wanted to call home. I decided to go assess them on my own: it was a long hike and maneuvering a canoe would be difficult with the whole crew on board. I needed to decide where we were going to live, while also factoring in the effort it would require getting in and out for the next few years.

Of the three, the obvious choice was the one that seemed to be the most conveniently located. It was right on the bank of a small, well-traveled Purus river. During the dry season there was still enough water for large boats to get up and down the Purus River, and during the rainy season it was a lot easier to get out if we needed to evacuate. A lake amphibian plane could easily land on that stretch of river and we would be able to exit with ease.

The first day of my assessment consisted of hiring a boat – well, three boats – to take me along with the tribal leaders to the various locations. This also happened to be where the current translators were doing all of their linguistic work, and it was also where a majority of the Indians were living because they wanted access to the outside world. This was really the only place that offered that.

But when I got there, my heart was unsettled. This wasn't where the Lord wanted us to live for the next two years. I shared this with the translation team and they understood. That meant I needed to choose between the other two locations.

Location number two was called Highland, a literal translation in English. They named it that simply because this area was slightly higher than the river and didn't flood during the rainy season. This is where the Paumari planted citrus trees and cashew trees, and some exotic Brazilian varieties of fruit trees. The people here had an interest in agriculture, and I was sure God would use my farming talents to minister to these people. It would be a perfect home base for us. We could set up a clinic and Betty could start a medical school to teach the Indians about basic medicines. It just felt right.

But the Lord had different plans.

As clearly as I heard God say *"No."* to site number one, I heard him say it again to site number two.

That left me with the third village, Chrispino. My friend, Chief Fari, was living there with his family. Because he was the chief of this group, he got to have the final say on whether we would even be allowed to live in that location – not that I was worried he would say no. Fari was excited that I had turned down the other two locations -- he knew I was going to pick his location as *home*.

I was not excited about location number three.

This was where the shaman had their training grounds. As we were walking from Highland to Chrispino, I was overwhelmed with a fear I'd never experienced before. As I walked, I felt like I was back on my survival hike, all alone, fear and anxiety permeating my entire being. I was nearly overwhelmed by my inner turmoil.

Is it safe to bring my family here? Here, where the witch doctors were going through training? Is it safe to bring my little babies here? Here, where there's a known pedophile roaming around the village? Is it safe for us to move into a location where we would have a hard time getting out unless it's the rainy season?

My worries were screaming into my ears. The longer I walked, the louder my fear and anxiety grew. Satan was after me.

I started to pray in English. The Indians don't speak a word of English so I had complete and total privacy. They knew

I was praying, but they didn't really understand. I pleaded with the Lord:

Show me, Father. Is this where you want me to bring my family?

After an hour and a half of hiking, my legs started to give out on me. They were weak and trembling -- I felt like a newborn colt. We'd been walking for hours so of course I was tired, but that wasn't the type of exhaustion I was feeling. This tiredness was deeper than physical exhaustion. This was spiritual warfare.

Satan was after me.

Joshua's words in Deuteronomy 31:6 popped into my head. The Holy Spirit reminded me of those words I'd memorized so many years before:

Be strong and courageous,
do not be afraid or tremble at them,
for the Lord your God is the one who goes with you.
He will not fail you or forsake you.

I thought, *Really? Thank you, Lord.*

I echoed this verse again and again as I reveled in this promise from Scripture.

The Lord is so gentle when we need Him, when we desperately ask Him to help us. He sent me a sign: a blue-morpho.

It's a butterfly with huge wingspan – probably five to eight inches across – and it's this beautifully vibrant fluorescent blue. It hovered right in front of my nose while I was walking, its wings tenderly fanning my face. Here I was, drenched and exhausted in the middle of the jungle, and the Lord was telling me, "Look, Dean, I will never leave or forsake you. I'm right here with you."

That butterfly stayed right there in front of my face, all the way until we reached site number three.

———

Chief Fari wanted me to live right next to him. I didn't know what he meant until he showed me exactly where he wanted me to build our house.

It was literally three feet from his.

He wanted to be able to jump from his house to mine without having to step in the mud. We would basically be living in a two-bedroom duplex. It's hot in the jungle, really hot. In order to avoid stifling any chance of airflow, the houses have no walls. If you were really wealthy, you might have a hammock, but most of these people didn't have that luxury. The houses were completely open and Fari wanted us to be right there with him.

I thought a little privacy sounded like a good idea.

I joked with Fari as best as my broken Portuguese allowed. I'm sure it was hilarious to witness me struggling through our negotiation, but eventually we agreed that I could build my house about 40 feet from his. I had a plan. I was going to introduce a new style of housing, and our home was going to be the model for it. I was going to show them how to build their houses out of jungle material and how to pick hardwoods that wouldn't rot in less than a year.

That night, the chief announced to his students that Dean and Betty, missionaries from the United States, were going to come and live with them in the village. I arranged for my family to return in several months so that I had time to pick up supplies, arrange transportation for bringing in building materials, and get anything else we needed in order to live in the village for six weeks at a time.

Before I left, I needed to hire about 40 men to help me with my building project. Some of them were young teens, others were what the Paumari considered *old*. Old is relative there, though. If you're celebrating your 50th birthday, you're extremely old. The infant mortality rate in this location is shockingly high -- it isn't uncommon to bury several babies each month.

My plan was to teach these guys how to build a split-level home using some material from the outside world, but I also wanted to teach them how to carefully pick hardwood timbers from the jungle to use, too. I wanted to teach them so that they could then go on and teach others in their tribe. I arranged to pick up some roofing materials, boards, and an abundance of nails.

The day we arrived on the boat was a memorable one. When we finally pulled up to the bank and started unloading materials, the Indians became incredibly excited. They had never seen building material like this. Very few of them had ever even come out to the city. It took about two days on a canoe going downstream, and it took seven days to get back going upstream against the swift current. Very few of them had any clue what I had brought with me.

The guys I'd hired when I was last there were eager to work for me again -- they knew I paid in cash instead of booze and clothes. I wanted to teach them basic math skills so they could count change and learn the value of money.

We loaded all of our stuff onto canoes so we could haul it back to the village – the water level was high enough that we could take a canoe all the way home. When we got there, we unloaded everything and had our first planning meeting that night.

We gathered in a circle and I talked to them in my best blend of Paumari-infused Portuguese. Fari grinned from ear to ear, enjoying every moment of my broken attempts at conversation. They laughed at me a couple of times when I pronounced things incorrectly, but they clearly understood what I was trying to explain – and I understood them. The relationships we had been building over the last couple of years were paying off.

They trusted us and we were starting to trust them.

We divided the hired crew of 40 men and boys into teams with specific assignments. We needed to go into the jungle and cut thatch that we could use as temporary roofing, and we needed to cut hardwood timbers that would become the primary structure of the house. We also needed to cut down some palm trees to make flooring -- if we removed the bark, it folded out similar to a tarp. Making a floor out of this made it really easy to clean your house, too. All you had to do was stomp your feet and the crumbs would fall through the little cracks in your flooring and your house was magically clean again.

My excitement grew with every delivery we brought in from the jungle -- we were going to build our new house. We piled everything up into specific stages that we would use in order to construct this project in a manner they could realize the next step of this building project. We quickly made ourselves a temporary shelter, more like a hut, to protect us from the constant rain that had already started. It was about as temporary of a home as we could get, but it would at least get my family out of the 24-hour Downpours. Our simple timbers, thatched roof and hammocks were so very comfortable after a long day of constructing our jungle house.

The Paumari were terribly confused when we started building the house. They couldn't wrap their heads around how we were constructing the building. They'd never built anything that would last longer than 6-8 months. They were baffled by the idea of my house having two floors – such intricacies were unheard of in their feeble structures.

I didn't want to hinder any semblance of coolness, so the wall on the inside of the house was only a half wall. The upper level also had a half wall so that we had somewhere to sleep and have at least a little bit of privacy. The bottom floor was communal: the Indians were always welcome to come spend time in our home.

This area also served as Betty's kitchen, and we eventually used it as our school.

The younger guys were so enamored with the design that they started building their own while we were still building mine. It was exciting to see the domino effect our efforts were having on the village. They were teaching each other. We finished building the house in less than a week. It felt great to carry in our few possessions -- we had our own little jungle home.

We had a meeting that first night in our new place. We tried to sing some Christian songs, but there were only a couple of Christians in the tribe at the time, so we sang some cultural Paumari songs, too. I also tried to read some Scripture in Portuguese since the New Testament hadn't been translated into their language yet. All in all, it ended up being a delightful evening of praising God for blessing and protecting us throughout this adventure.

The mortality rate in this particular area was horrendous. Not only were babies dying, but so were the adults. Aside from the natural ramifications of living out in the middle of the jungle, they were mostly dying from drinking filthy water. The water supply became especially toxic during the dry season because they would bathe and go to the bathroom in the same stream they drank from. This was also where they soaked manioc, an incredibly poisonous potato-like root. With all of this filth mucking up the water, it was no surprise the Paumari were experiencing all kinds of gastrointestinal issues. They were suffering liver failure, stomach pain, and horrible intestinal complications.

Burying all of these people – our friends – was becoming a heavy weight to bear.

Father, show me what to do. How can I help these people?

One day, while I was having my quiet time, I stumbled upon a solution. I was praying for the Lord to show me an easy way to gather and store clean water somewhere close to the village. Then I saw it.

Right in front of me was a natural bend in the stream. Immediately, I saw potential to build a dam there that would create a pool of clean water. It would be so easy to carry water from there to the village.

I called Fari to my house to share my idea. We called for a meeting with all of the men in two days. I know this seems like a long time to wait, but it's not like we could text the rest of the Paumari to tell them we needed to have a meeting. Fari had to send runners to all of the different village locations to invite them to the meeting "Gino" was calling.

There was an incredible turnout -- the men were eager to hear about my plan. It was obvious to me that my efforts to build solid relationships had been successful.

I explained why I wanted to find a clean water supply for them and broke down the different ways it would enhance their quality of life. I implemented all of the skills I learned while working for Fruehauf Trailer Company in Denver and tried my best to get them to buy in to what I knew was a necessary change to their way of life. I needed them to take ownership of this project -- it couldn't just be something the missionary was doing. If they didn't own it, the dam would die a certain death after my family had departed.

They needed to feel personally responsible for the upkeep of this dam. It would have to be rebuilt again and again after the rainy season washed it out, and they needed to fervently uphold this as tradition.

We scheduled a start date and had a strong group of men ready to help. The stream was probably 20 to 25 feet wide and we slowly started creating our dam. We used a lot of soil and as many rocks as we could possibly find – after all, it's a tough job putting fresh soil into a running stream.

There were probably three or four other guys working with me in the middle of the stream. We'd been at it for a while when our progress came to a screeching halt.

I spotted a snake swimming right at me.

I abhor snakes, so of course, my natural inclination was to eliminate the beast. I happened to be holding a shovel. With one swift motion, I slammed the shovel over its head and killed the snake. I felt rather proud of myself -- one swing and I finished him.

As soon as the men realized the snake was dead, they fled.

What just happened? I was protecting them,
doing the right thing.

Apparently, I had just made a huge mistake.

It was a long, lonely walk back to the village. The dam wasn't completed and I couldn't finish on my own -- I needed the Paumari to help. But they weren't even talking to me and I had absolutely no idea why. I would pass my "friends" on the trail and they would turn their faces away, refusing to even look at me.

Father, show me what I've done. What did I say?
What did I do? Show me how I offended my friends.

It was obvious I had committed some sort of grievous sin against them, but I had absolutely no idea what it was. After several days, Fari came to our little house. With a stern and angry look on his face he said, "Gino, I need to talk to you." I knew it wasn't going to be good news, but I was desperate to know what I had done and how I could fix the damage that had been done over the last couple of agonizing weeks.

Very seriously, he explained to me, "Gino, when you killed that snake, you killed the spirit that's going to bring us water. Now my people are going to die."

I tried to help him understand, "Fari, the water doesn't come from the snake spirit. It comes from the Lord, our loving heavenly Father. Killing that snake did not kill the water that will keep your people alive."

I tried my best to explain God's provision and God's love for us. I tried to tell him about God's forgiveness of our sins. I don't think he understood -- he had been worshipping the spirits for all of his life, and now, all of a sudden, this missionary from Denver comes in and starts saying that there's a God who loves him. That isn't something you latch onto in a single conversation.

We never did finish that dam project, but Fari and I continued to have deeper and deeper spiritual conversations.

———

The majority of our time in the village was spent getting to know the Paumari. In order to build relationships with them, to build their trust, we needed to spend quality time immersing ourselves in their world. Early one Sunday evening we were doing just that.

A few of the Indians had come over to our house and we were just sitting around chitchatting, building our Paumari vocabulary. I was enjoying listening to their humor when a Brazilian from upriver walked into the village.

We had never met this guy before and as he walked into the village clearing I heard him ask, "Is the missionary here?"

The Indians excitedly replied, "Yes! He's right over there," and showed him to our house.

As he approached, I got up and greeted him with a warm Brazilian welcome. As appropriate in Brazilian culture, I offered him a drink of cool water. Since our house wasn't located near the river, he probably had to hike for two hours after getting out of his boat.

He was unnervingly anxious. There was an envelope tucked

into his hand that was soaked from the sweat of his palms. The sender had scrawled my name in very sloppy penmanship, *Gino*.

As I read the letter, my heart became very heavy.

The man delivering the letter worked as a servant for a Patron who owned an exorbitant amount of land near this particular village. He was furious that we were working with the Paumari, that we had the audacity to teach them basic math and construction skills. We were ruining his slave-like relationship with the Paumari men.

He would often hire them to cut lumber and rubber for him. Instead of paying them with actual currency, he would give them liquor. The more intoxicated they got, the more he would charge them for the booze. Once they were completely inebriated, he would issue them a "worker's loan."

Most of the Paumari men were deeply in debt after one weekend of binge drinking.

The letter was short and to the point. In translated English it read:

> *Gino, unless you leave the village now I will kill you*
> *Monday morning.*

The Indian men sitting next to me saw the clouds move across my face and pleaded with me to read the letter to them. I was torn: part of me wanted to read them the letter and to tell them of the threat on my life, but part of me wanted to keep it private.

I excused myself and went to talk with Betty who was having a great time communicating with the women. Immediately, she got down on her knees and prayed, "Father, show us what to do. Give us wisdom and help us not to react to this threat."

Together, we decided that we should share the letter with our Paumari friends. As I read the letter, the chief became very angry – his protective nature had ferociously kicked in. He was preparing for battle. I said, "Fari, relax. We serve a living God, a God who can protect us, and we are not going to be afraid."

He couldn't understand what I meant and kept asking, "Why don't you want to fight? All I need to do is give my people the command and they will go and kill this evil man!"

II Samuel 22:2-3:

> *...The Lord is my rock and my fortress and my deliverer;*
> *My God, my rock, in whom I take refuge, my shield and the*
> *horn of my salvation, my stronghold and my refuge; My*
> *savior, You save me from violence.*

This passage was a fierce reminder for us during these troubling times. There were still moments when I thought it would be a good idea for us to take this threat seriously, that we should leave and never come back. But that's not what the Lord had commanded us to do, so we decided to stay and continue to work. We prayed fervently for strength from the Lord and we did not yield to the threat.

It wasn't but a couple of days later and we received another message from the same Patron.

This message couldn't have been more different than the first.

His son was dying of malaria and he needed me to help him. This Patron, the same one that had threatened my life just a few days ago, was now asking for me to save the life of his son. He begged me to arrange to have our airplane come and land on the river to take his son into a town with a hospital. He was afraid that the malaria was taking his son's life.

So, we did just that.

We sent an Indian downstream to go to the nearest little town and contact the police department who could then send a message back to the Wycliffe Center. I had written a simple note requesting the Wycliffe/JAARS pilot to fly into a near-by lake to pick up this dying young man. It would then be about a two-hour flight to the nearest hospital.

His son made a full recovery – praise God. He protected my life, and my family, and He manifested his healing power for this unbelieving, angry Patron in the process.

Psalm 4:8

> *In peace I will both lie down and sleep, for You alone,*
> *O Lord, make me to dwell in safety.*

XII
A Change in Perspective

As missionaries, it was our job to go into these different tribal locations and teach the natives. Our entire mission was to improve the quality of life for these people by bringing supplies, knowledge, and the Word of God into their homes. We would go into the different tribal areas thinking we had a plan, but we always seemed to also end up being the students.

One time, our son went fishing – he loved to fish – and on this occasion he caught a beautiful fish. I don't recall what kind of fish it was, but it had this incredibly sharp, spiny fin. Our son was young, probably only around seven or eight years old at the time, and when he was handling the fish, somehow its barb found itself stuck right through the middle of his hand.

Naturally, he immediately burst into tears. This fish was still alive and kept flopping around with its fin stuck straight through his hand. He was bleeding, terrified, and in a lot of pain.

Betty and I stood there, utterly astounded by what had just happened right in front of our eyes. The sight of it was disturbing. We stood there in shock as we tried to figure out how on earth we could get the fin out of his hand without ripping his skin and flesh.

I quickly ran to get my pliers so that I could pull that fin out of his hand.

Fari was also there and had been watching the entire ordeal play out. He stopped me just before I took action. "Gino, let me help you."

Calmly, Fari pulled out his little knife. He nimbly cuts the fish on the inside of our son's soft hand, goes to the top and gently pulls out the fin.

The absolute opposite of what I wanted to do.

I wanted to yank it out. I wanted to retrieve it from his hand. I wanted to abolish the fin from my precious child's hand in the most expedient way possible.

What I didn't realize, though, was that this fin had barbs. If I had done what I wanted, it would have ripped his hand to shreds. My instincts would have caused him serious, lifelong damage.

Instead, Fari removed the fish with minimal effort and very little damage.

I needed to be the student.

Fari knew things that I did not know. He had a whole host of knowledge about the jungle that I simply didn't have. He taught me so many things – not just about the jungle, but about life. His cultural differences and outlook on life greatly expanded my own understanding of the world. Not only did the Lord use Betty and me to teach Fari about Him, but He also used Fari to teach us how to see the world from a very different perspective.

XIII
Jungle Stingray

In Brazilian culture (especially in the indigenous tribes) people take long lunch breaks taking upwards of two to three hours. One day, we were coming in from the fields after working hard to clear an area to grow rice. We desperately needed a break to cool off and to get a drink of fresh water. On days like these, we would often congregate and take a rest together if we took a break close to lunch time. In such a harsh place with such oppressive heat, your body needs rest after difficult work out in the unrelenting sun.

On this particular day, my wife, Betty, had fixed lunch for us to all enjoy as a family. This was typically a great time for us to go down to the river and wash dishes. It's incredibly difficult to maneuver the riverbank to get into the water and wash dishes, so we only did it one time a day. We would save our dirty dishes from the night before and lump them with our breakfast and lunch dishes from that day's meals. This was typically a family activity, but I was spending my two-hour break doing some language learning with the chief, my instructor. I was diligently occupied with learning conversational language, busy in the work of grasping new concepts, terms, and new moments of joy and pain, when I heard a ghastly scream – a desperate plea for help.

Instantly, I recognized that this was my dear Betty's voice. Fari and I leapt from our seats and sprinted down to the river to find Betty in utter agony. She was sitting on the side of the riverbank with our little daughter. Our baby was sobbing while her mother screamed in pain. For the life of me, I couldn't figure out what happened – I just saw that her foot was covered in blood. I thought,

> *My goodness! She must've stepped on something*
> *or cut her foot in some way.*

I tried and tried to rinse off her foot, but the blood just kept pouring.

Without any hesitation, Fari said that she had been hit by a stingray. I said, "Stingray? This isn't saltwater – we're in the middle of the jungle! This is fresh water." Fari informed us that occasionally we have stingrays in this area if the water is excessively high, and that their hit is extremely poisonous. We carried my sweet bride up to the house, while she continued to be in excruciating pain.

My specialty is certainly not in the medical field. I am a Business and Organizational Leadership guy and in no way am I a connoisseur of healthcare. Once we got away from the water, Betty asked me to bring the clinic crate to her side – I had built a little portable clinic so we could take it in and out of villages. Though I was desperately trying to help my wife, I was having a terrible time trying not to faint. I tried my best to carefully clean the wound and wrap bandages around the cut to stop – or at least temper – the bleeding. Betty gave me step-by-step instructions on the different injections she had brought from the pharmacy back in Porto Velho, but nothing seemed to work. In spite of our efforts, the swelling had already started and her fever was quickly rising.

We didn't sleep that night.

I prayed. Oh, my goodness, did I pray. And we prayed together. Our children were distraught that their mama was hurting. I felt utterly helpless. *Psalms 34:18 "the Lord is close to the brokenhearted and saves those who are crushed in spirit"* perfectly embodies how I felt on that dark, hopeless day.

> *What am I going to do? I feel so dependent on you,*
> *Father. I don't know what to do.*

I knew my wife was feeling worse with each moment that passed. The swelling was unceasing and I was horribly aware that we were going to be facing some sort of life-threatening infection. I remember thinking of another passage in *Psalms*

147:3 "he heals the brokenhearted and binds up their wounds."

But, Father, would you please bring healing to Betty's foot?

We awoke the next morning and I knew that something – anything – had to be done. She was getting worse. She couldn't walk at all. She was sitting on one of the little lawn chairs (we had brought some down on one of our previous trips), and I brought her up buckets of water to give her a quick shower to temporarily relieve her ailing body of her sweltering fever. I knew that I had no choice but to go for help. I desperately prayed in the name of Jesus, begging for him to please show me what to do.

Suddenly, I remembered another mission organization had purchased a floating clinic and that they had plans to go up and down the river to offer medical help to the national Brazilians. At this point, I felt like I had absolutely no other choice than to hike out to the river and *hope* that they had docked near us. I left Fari's wife to care for my Betty and my babies, and I made arrangements to have a guide take me up to the river to a possible location the missionary group had mentioned as a great place for them to dock their clinic.

It was a long, unbelievably hot trip, and I felt like this plan was a catastrophic mistake. But, then, the Lord reminded me of a verse: *Psalms 73:26, "my flesh and my heart may fail but God is the strength of my heart and my portion forever."*

And I knew that I was only able to endure this miserable trip, this miserable heartache, because God's strength was becoming mine.

I arrived at the river and carefully maneuvered a borrowed canoe to where I *hoped* we would spot the floating clinic.

Hallelujah!

We could see the clinic boat in the distance. With what little energy we had left, we paddled as fast as we could to reach that blessed boat. I explained to the acting nurse what had happened and she gave me medicine, antibiotics, and other injections. I had no idea whether or not this was the right medicine, but at that point I was willing to try anything. The nurse attempted to encourage me with less than encouraging words, "The injections I gave you, along with all of the other medicines and instructions – I'm not sure they'll work."

Here I am, in the middle of the Amazon jungle, at my very wit's end. Again, the Lord came to my rescue and reminded me of Psalms 55:22, "cast your cares on the Lord and he will sustain you. He will never let the righteous fall." I held fast to that promise and said:

> *Lord, please don't let my wife die.*
> *Please, Father, allow this medicine to help.*

We hastily began our journey back. We tried to go as fast as we possibly could, but before we knew it we realized that our journey had already taken an entire day just getting to the clinic. Now we also had to maneuver the canoe upstream in the dark. The river current was viciously swift. We would paddle as hard as we humanly could, only to make abysmally slow progress. But I would not – could not – let that distract me from my journey. I was determined to get that healing medicine into Betty's body as fast as possible.

Fourteen hours later, we finally arrived at our little location. Her condition had drastically worsened. The infection had spread even further while I was gone. Her wound was garishly haunting to me, her fever was high enough that Betty had begun to hallucinate. Together I prayed with the Paumari:

If it's time for my wife to enter the hands of Jesus, please, God, don't make her suffer any more.

John 14: 3-4

And if I go and prepare a place for you, I will come again and will take you to myself, that where I am you may be also. And you know the way to where I am going.

I was able to share this in the Paumari language. I didn't have a clue as to what the Indians were actually hearing, but I was certain that we were preparing to lose my wife, the mother to my children, and their friend, right there in the jungles of Brazil. I felt like Mary and Martha when they told Jesus that Lazarus was sick and was dying. I always read

Jesus' response as being a nonchalant, "okay, I'll come," and then He delayed and took his sweet time to actually arrive at their house. In that moment, I knew how Mary and Martha must have felt. Their emotional response was exactly how I felt: the Lord was running out of time.

Fari, together with his wife, had become our special friends, and our kids had also become incredibly close as they played together every day. I was in utterly excruciating pain emotionally, trying to console my distraught children, and I will never forget how the Chief and his family spent that night crying, weeping for my sweet bride.

Fari was performing some of his witchcraft sacrifices in his hut right next to our house. I pleaded with him not to come into our house, but my prayer didn't seem to be working. At the same time, I felt like the Lord was prompting me to continue praying and somehow this would be a beautiful opportunity for Him to show his power – His plan just didn't seem to include this beauty right at that point.

I remember walking out on a fallen tree, as far as I could, then looking back toward our house with a dying wife suffering in absolute pain. It was tragically symbolic -- I felt like I was at the end of my rope. We had made standing arrangements with the pilots who were servicing the Wycliffe missionaries to give us a mail drop any time they were flying over any of the different villages where the translators were. I found myself standing out there on this tree, feeling so alone. I had no idea what day of the week it was – was it even a weekday? I was so terribly alone.

There was no way for me to send a text message or an email to our friends and supporters back in the United States. We didn't even have radio contact there: I had no way to connect with them, so I prayed,

> *Holy Spirit would you please prompt them to pray*
> *for us at this very moment.*

Minutes later, I heard this beautiful, glorious sound: a Cessna 206. I will never forget the sound of this aircraft coming toward our location, knowing that we're getting a mail drop, and that somehow, someway there's going to be some answers to our prayers in this mail. The plane was flying rather high, but, sure enough, the pilot was circling our little village to signal that he was preparing to drop our mail. You see, we had already been in this particular jungle location for several weeks so I was excited not only to get mail, but I just knew that there would be an answer to all of our prayers. I knew that somehow the Lord was going to reveal himself through this mail drop – either through someone from the states having sent us something, or by providing some other divine solution to this dire situation.

It was a moment of *hope*.

The Indians heard the same thing I had, and they came sprinting out to the small clearing in the middle of the jungle. The plane's target area is very small, so the pilots would normally come as low as they could and drop it right out the side window. But today he was staying high, much higher than normal, preparing for the drop. All indications aside, I knew we were indeed getting some kind of drop when I faintly saw him open the window and drop out a package.

I'm not exactly sure what happened, but somehow, as he was dropping the package out the window, it caught on some sharp edge – perhaps the latch from the window, I'm not sure what – but it ripped the package. All of our mail was floating down like little feathers, fluttering through the air. What started as a moment of absolute joy and excitement quickly turned into complete and utter despair. My heart sank with disbelief and disappointment.

Lord, what are you doing?

The Indians ran into the jungle, desperately trying to retrieve any letters and papers that were now getting stuck in the tree tops – I joined them in this seemingly fruitless endeavor.

We did find some invoices and bills from our monthly expenses, but there was absolutely nothing that even came close to answers to our prayers for Betty.

I just felt so alone.

I couldn't even communicate with the pilot – someone who could then communicate via telephone back to America to inform our supporting churches. It was like I'd had this moment of joy, of ecstasy, and then I was just right back down into complete despair. I remember fixing dinner for the kids that night, trying as best as I could to hold the family together. They were terribly concerned about their Momma's pain. The fever was beginning to come down slightly but it was still extremely high. She had stopped hallucinating and seemed lucid enough to have short conversations with us.

A few days later she seemed to give us indication that she was doing a little better. After consulting with some of the Paumari men, we decided to make a homemade stretcher and see if we could carry her out to the river. The water level had dropped somewhat, making it impossible to get the canoe from the location where we were living out to the river. We would have to carry her over ground for several hours – now, that was a long hike without much conversation.

Our hearts were too heavy to talk.

We finally arrived at the river bank and waited for a boat, praise the Lord.

Philippians 4:6: Do not be anxious about anything but in everything by prayer and petition with Thanksgiving present your requests to God and the peace of God which transcends all understanding will guard your hearts and your mind in Christ Jesus.

He was beginning to answer prayer in a way that I hadn't expected. We didn't have to wait long before we saw a boat going down the river. We waved the jungle sign, begging the boat pilot to pull over and stop. Straining to use my very best Portuguese, I shared with them what was going on. They said, "Certainly, you can ride with us." We boarded his boat and headed back down to this little town called Labrea.

Even though my wife was still suffering, and was in visibly excruciating pain, our arrival did not induce any change in course for the river traders. They make their income by travelling up and down the river, so we frequently stopped in order for them to trade for jungle fruits and raw rubber. When the traders were hungry, they pulled the boat over to the riverbank, tied it to a tree, and hiked into the jungle to find something to eat. If a national flagged them down, they would bargain a trade for some product.

And so our journey went on. It took us hours and hours and hours to finally get to a location where we could finally arrange for a flight out to the city of Porto Velho.

When we finally did arrive, I hired several of the guys from the boat to help me carry Betty up the riverbank. We then contacted a local pastor of a small national church and asked him if I could stay with them until I could make arrangements for a flight back to the Center.

Flights in the jungle are completely different than what we are used to in the U.S. Daily flights are not feasible in the interior of the jungle, and the company that served this tiny town would typically only fly once or twice a week – providing they had passengers or were contracted to fly in food and product for the locals. Thankfully, the airport controller did have radio contact, so I asked for them to please call in a request for a plane to come get us and take us to Porto Velho, where Betty could finally get some medical care. She had become alarmingly weak and was no longer able to even communicate with our children.

We stayed with the Pastor and his family for several more days while we waited.

At last, the airport sent a runner to inform us that the plane was *finally* on the way and would be landing in two hours. Immediately, I made arrangements with several of the men from the Pastor's church to help me carry Betty and our children to the airport to anxiously await our flight.

By this point, Betty's infection had again become really nasty. We were greeted by an ambulance when we landed in Porto Velho and she was immediately swept away to a local hospital. The doctor carefully examined Betty's infected wound and asked me to consider amputation. I begged him, "please don't, please don't. We believe in a God that heals, in a God that restores."

Together Betty and I prayed and prayed, eventually finding ourselves joined by other missionaries from several different missionary agencies who also prayed for Jesus to heal her infection that started at her foot and was now moving up her leg. One night, a fellow missionary living at the Wycliffe Center was prompted by the Holy Spirit to pray through the night, all the way into morning.

Betty woke me before sunrise, saying, "Dean, I feel better, something happened during the night."

God was healing her infection – the pain was finally starting to slowly recede. After many weeks of recovery and therapy, Betty was able to walk with limited pain. We undeniably experienced the healing power of Jesus, just as Mary and Martha witnessed when Jesus brought Lazarus back from death.

This experience will forever shape how I look at the incredible power of prayer and the joy of having an army of prayer warriors who are committed to listening to the Holy Spirit and committed to praying until they hear from God.

XIV
Apurrina

Have you ever said to yourself, "What on earth am I doing? Why am I doing this?"

I found myself wallowing in this very sentiment when we visited yet *another* tribal location approximately an hour's flight away from our primary assignment with the Paumari. We had been asked to spend some time with this group, primarily to teach them how to plant, grow, and harvest rice and corn.

With no avenues for communication other than sending runners, we left for this particular visit completely unsure whether the Indians would even be in this location at this particular time.

The thing about living in the jungle – also known as the Rain Forest – is that life pretty much revolves around water. In those few weeks when it doesn't rain every single day, it is crucial to plan for the planting and harvesting that needs to happen in the fleeting cease-fire of rain.

In order for me to teach them the techniques and procedures of planting and harvesting, it was imperative that I showed up at the just the right time in their water calendar.

When we arrived at this tribal location, we found that most of the men had left on a major hunting trip. The women were there, but they had no idea when the men would return.

In my own life, time management is incredibly high on my list of priorities – it has been that way my whole life. When I make a commitment to be at a meeting or a conference, or I promise somebody I'm going to help them, you better believe that I will be there and I will be there *on time*.

I remember sitting on a bucket in our little hut while the rain outside was pouring down in sheets. I thought to myself, "Why am I here?" I felt like the children of Israel when they had left Egypt. A short distance of travelling later and they were mumbling and grumbling, trying to convince themselves that living in Egypt wasn't all that bad. They'd already started to fondly remember the leeks and garlic – all of the attractive parts of Egypt were becoming more alluring by the hour.

I couldn't help but think just how marvelous it would be if I was back in Denver, enjoying the cool fall season, people walking around speaking my mother tongue.

I was having myself a pity party.

I'm sitting on my bucket stewing when I suddenly realize that I'm acting like Jonah. God asked him to deliver a message he didn't want to give, when finally, reluctantly Jonah obeyed. In spite of all his complaining, the Lord intervened on Jonah's behalf.

That was me.

I was longing for an opportunity to attend a time management workshop, desperate for a day planner that was filled to the brim with activities. But that simply wasn't reality. I felt an intense loneliness while I waited for those men to return from their hunting trip. I found my mind drifting to Philippians 3:7-11.

But whatever gain I had, I counted as loss for the sake of Christ. Indeed, I count everything as loss because of the surpassing worth of knowing Christ Jesus my Lord. For his sake I have suffered the loss of all things and count them as rubbish, in order that I may gain Christ and be found in him, not having a righteousness of my own that comes from the law, but what comes through faith in Christ, the righteousness from God that depends on faith – that I may know him and the power of his resurrection, and may share his sufferings, becoming like him in his death, that by any means possible I may attain the resurrection from the dead.

I'm sitting there feeling sorry for myself only to realize I wasn't there for me. I was there because the Lord had clearly asked us to serve in the jungles of Brazil.

The men did finally return from their hunting trip – an extremely successful one at that. They were able to gather enough food to feed the entire village for nearly a week.

While I was sitting on my bucket, fussing and complaining because I felt like the Lord's timing was off - that mine was better - the Lord was truly protecting and providing for his people.

If you find yourself questioning your purpose – your ability to hear God's voice, your sense of knowing what to do, God's call for your life – I challenge you to read Psalm 63:1-4.

O God, you are my God; earnestly I seek you; my soul thirsts for you; my flesh faints for you, as in a dry and weary land where there is no water. So I have looked upon you in the sanctuary, beholding your power and glory. Because your steadfast love is better than life, my lips will praise you. So I will bless you as long as I live; in your name I will lift up my hands.

XV

The Brazilian Fishing Style Guide

Fishing is one of the most sustainable forms of hunting in the Amazon jungle. Especially during the low-water season, it was a fairly low-risk way to find food (compared to hunting amidst the big cats and Tapirs), and it was easy prey to prepare. One of the tastiest fish you could catch was a Piranha – and that is coming from a guy who does not like fish.

I know what you're thinking: *Piranhas? They're so dangerous. How do you keep them from eating your hand when you try to get them off of the line?*

But, let me tell you, Piranhas are probably one of the greatest misconceptions the civilized world has about the jungle. They are nothing like the sensationalized bloodthirsty monsters portrayed in movies.

You still must be awake and alert as you wade through the rivers, but it's not like they are going to come and chomp your leg off out of nowhere. During what we called the "dry season," when it only rained once a day, we would try to clear out the streams when the water would recede. Being able to get in and out was important, so during this brief window of time, we would go in and clear out the debris that had fallen and cut a path for the canoes.

A lot of the large fallen trees would require hours of chopping with an axe, some had been down for several years and we needed to take them out. In order to clear a path, we actually had to get into the water: it's not something we could do from a canoe. We would send out a scout party of native Indians to survey the water around the fallen trees before everyone started the process of removing the debris.

They had a way of knowing where Piranhas would be nesting and whenever I saw a Piranha jump out of the water quickly, I knew to quickly get back in the boat. Other than that, we would spend the whole day in the water. I honestly do not even remember a single incident where Betty had to treat a Piranha injury – we just had to be careful.

When you fish for Piranha, all you need is a cloth – a t-shirt of some kind of material – to hold the fish. They aren't going to attack you, but they do have sharp teeth. So, you just wrap your hand up to protect it from their sharp teeth and remove the line like you would for any other fish.

However, they did like to bite through the fish line. In a flash, your line would be completely useless. In order to stop them from doing this, we would take tin can lids and wrap the around the string so that when they would start snapping at it, they'd bite the tin instead of the line.

I went fishing for Piranha with my dear friend Fari one day. We went to a spot that was notorious for having Piranha – they were consistently easier to catch in some places. We had been fishing for a while and absolutely nothing was biting.

Not even turtles.

I like to have fun; I enjoy joking. Fari and I were sitting there in our little dugout canoe and it's starting to get hot. Jungle hot. I had some great food waiting for me back at the house – Spam. But he didn't, so we really did need to come home with some fish. We were sitting here in this little canoe and I don't know what possessed me to say this, but it just came out of my head. "Fari, I know why the fish aren't biting."

Fari is a shaman, okay? He's basically in charge of everyone and everything in this part of the jungle. He is the leader. Fari responds to me, "Gino, why?"

Completely deadpan, I said, "We have to whistle."

I'm not even sure I had the right word for whistle – I think I did – and he looked at me like I was absolutely crazy.

I said, "No, Fari! You have to go…" and I began to whistle a merry little fishing tune.

And a fish bit.

Oh no. What have I done?

Fari, the shaman, was taken aback by my abilities, and I could tell he was thinking *This guy has some powers.* In a way, my joke had come back around to bite me.

Not too long ago, one of my sons was out fishing and the fish weren't biting.

So he started whistling my merry fishing tune.

XVI
Karatiana

On several occasions, Betty and I were honored with the opportunity to work with a tribe referred to as the Karatiana. The linguists for this tribal group had come from London to work on the task of translating the New Testament into their mother tongue. They had just completed the first draft of the Gospel of Luke when they unexpectedly had to go back to London due to some extreme health issues. They were so disappointed that they wouldn't be able to personally deliver the first printed copy of Luke to the Karatiana.

They reached out to us and asked if we would please deliver a copy of their rough draft. They also asked us to spend some quality time helping their language workers who they had been able to teach how to read the Karatiana language to some extent.

We were taking the first printed copy of Scripture into a tribe that had *never* held the Holy Word of God in their hands. This was a sacred honor and we were beyond elated to be part of that joyous moment.

Excitement was building among the Karatiana. They had heard that there was a special delivery coming their way, that we were bringing them something very special.

I remember sitting there, listening to the chief stumble through those first few verses in Luke 1. Slowly, deliberately, he tried to pronounce the words. I couldn't understand one word of it, but his ineloquent reading was the most beautiful music. Seeing their faces filled with joy and gratitude over a stack of simple computer paper that was merely a rough draft of Scripture is a sight I will never forget.

———

After we had been there for a little while, I started to notice some projects within the community that we could get involved in and hopefully observe an improvement to their physical and spiritual needs. Betty was already picturing a clinic where we could treat the sick while teaching them to carry on after we would leave.

There was a river running right through the middle of the village and the bridge they'd constructed to cross it couldn't have been more treacherous. They would cut large trees to lay across the water and walk over the river on those rotting monstrosities. It was dumbfounding to watch them walk on those things. They could carry heavy loads – usually they had their babies tucked in a basket tied to their backs – and even if the tree was almost completely submerged in water, they would still cross with ease. It was a real-life circus act out there, watching them effortlessly scurry across their deadly high-wire.

As I breathlessly watched them day by day, I kept picturing a sturdy, safe bridge where they could walk without putting their lives in jeopardy – even in the rainy season.

There was an entrepreneur from the United States that had designed a portable sawmill and had shipped it to Brazil so that we could use it for times like this. This sawmill was designed to be broken down into small sections so that it could be taken out to the jungle. We could position the saw over a fallen tree and cut it into boards without ever needing to move it.

It was a brilliant concept.

I made plans to disassemble the saw into 3 ½ foot sections so that we could put it inside of a Cessna 206. I arranged for several flights to be made out to the tribe to move all of this mill out to the Karatiana village, since the plane wouldn't be able to carry the entire mill in a single trip.

The morning of, our family was on the first flight out and we got to enjoy watching the pilot fly back and forth for the rest of the day. It was delightful to watch him take off on those trips, knowing that there were helpers back in Porto Velho that would help him get the next piece every time he landed. Many, many 45-minute flights later and we finally had all of the pieces right there on the airstrip in the Karatiana village.

It was nearly dark by the time we had gotten everything hauled into the village. The pilot really wanted to go back that evening instead of spending the night and going back in the morning. In order to do so, he needed to take care of some important safety inspections first. Before he could take off, he needed to walk the entire airstrip to make sure there wasn't anything that would damage the aircraft during takeoff. This was something we should have been doing in between each flight during the day, but we were in a time crunch and we didn't do this as carefully as we probably should have.

Since it was his last trip and he had an empty plane, the pilot wanted to make sure no detail was ignored, so he decided to personally walk the strip before he took off. I walked with him and we spent our inspection time visiting, praying, and just talking about how amazing that day had been. We spent a lot of our time praising God for the saw mill we had just successfully delivered piece by piece. I couldn't wait to get started on putting it together the next day.

We were on our way back from walking the strip when we stopped dead in our tracks.

There was a massive hole in the ground.

Since it constantly rains in the jungle, the ground is always soft. As the plane would touch down during landing, an indentation would be made in the dirt where the wheels first touched the ground. Inches from the indentation where our plane had been landing with maximum cargo loads was a ginormous hole covered with grass. They had removed a tree stump there at some point and the dirt had settled over time into a three-feet wide, eight inches deep crater. Had the pilot landed his plane mere inches earlier, it would have certainly ended in a terrible death.

But God protected him – and our mission.

I Samuel 2:8-9

> ...*For the foundations of the earth are the Lord's;*
> *on them he has set the world.*
> *He will guard the feet of his faithful servants...*

Thankfully, His promise extends to the wheels of a Cessna 206.

———

We got the mill assembled and wheeled it out into the jungle to start cutting trees. It had tires, so we could just maneuver it to wherever we needed to go. I took a large number of men and boys with me on this maiden voyage: I planned on turning this into a training experience for some of them so that they could start teaching each other on their own.

They were all so excited they could hardly stand it.

We cut a beautiful, tall, straight tree, and after trimming some of the nearby brush and branches, we positioned the mill over the tree. I was determined to train the Karatiana how to do everything I was doing. Ideally, I wanted to see the men and boys I taught go on to teach their peers the skills they had learned. In Western Christian vernacular, this is what we called *discipleship training*: training others to train others.

This mill was powered by a ten-horsepower gasoline motor and I had planned my supply of fuel out so that I would have enough to complete our training program. Before I started the engine for the first time, I went over some safety precautions with the Indians and explained to them what exactly I was going to be doing. I tried to forewarn them about what the engine was going to sound like. The only engine they'd ever heard before belonged to the airplane that had delivered this mill to their village.

I was talking to them in Portuguese and they were trying their best to decipher what I was saying since I wasn't talking to them in their mother tongue. Finally, I wrapped the cord around the starter pulley and gave it a yank. It started up just like it was supposed to.

The noise was deafening.

They scattered, utterly terrified by the disturbance.

I waited a few minutes and, slowly but surely, they timidly returned to see if everything was okay. After I finally got them calmed down, we all had a good laugh about how scared they got over a loud hunk of metal.

After all of the brouhaha was finally over, it was time to cut. When the first board fell off the mill ramp, the Indians hooted in raucous excitement. Within minutes, we cut some beautiful boards. They were carrying them back to the village as fast as we could cut them.

Unbeknownst to me, they had already created a plan amidst themselves about who would receive the first batch of boards and what they would use them for. I was under the impression that I – the initiator of this new building project – would have some autonomy concerning how it would be distributed and used, but I quickly realized that I needed to yield to Karatiana culture. We had learned about how to handle these kinds of issues back in our SIL classes at the University of Oklahoma. If we wanted to create change, we first needed to listen. We needed to build trust with people before we started introducing our American culture and values.

There's nothing but trees out in the jungle, a supply of wood plentiful enough to build both houses and bridges. We cut wood for several weeks straight until we ran out of gas. At that point, we had cut enough wood to build a bridge *and* some ramps so they could carry in mud to cure and make bricks for more permanent houses.

Fast forward to today, and this tribe produces and transports product out of their village in the jungle to sell to the national market within 100 miles of their location.

———

This village was also the location of our first home-schoolroom. Wycliffe had a school at the Center that was taught by English-speaking teachers who were serving in Brazil as short-term missionaries, but we wanted to keep our sweet babies with us as much as possible - it was hard on us to leave them back at the Center.

On one occasion my wife agreed to be the teacher and we decided to make our schoolroom away from the house. By moving it out of our home, Betty would have an easier time establishing herself as *teacher* instead of *mama*. We were certainly not home-schooling professionals, but we did the best we possibly could.

It was incredibly challenging.

Our time in the jungle gave me an undeniable respect for teachers – that is *hard* work. If you're a teacher, please know that I have the utmost appreciation for you.

XVII
Mura Piraha

Early one morning, I had just finished caring for the Wycliffe team's dairy herd and was getting ready to walk back to our house across the Center to grab some breakfast. Betty had just completed her rounds in the area up and down the river where she had been providing medical care and assessments for people with various illnesses.

It was a normal day for us, or so we thought.

All of a sudden there was a man running as fast as he could up the road towards the Center. It was Dan, a translator who, together with his wife, had been assigned to translate the Scripture into the Mura Piraha language in the interior of Brazil.

Totally out of breath, he sprinted toward me, all the while saying, "Dean, help me. Dean, please help me!"

I tried my best to calm him down, but to no avail. At last, he caught his breath and started to talk in a voice I could actually understand. "My wife is dying from malaria. She is laying in the shade down at the riverbank unable to move. Our kids are down there with her, but we need to move quickly. We spotted a few snakes near the water, but I can't carry her. Dean she is dying and I need help!"

I raced into the office and began making calls. First, Betty, then some guys to help us carry her to an awaiting pickup so we could take her to the small interior hospital in Porto Velho.

My wife had already snatched up her medical backpack, jumped on our bike, and was hustling to the aid of our dear friend. Soon after, a bunch of us guys hopped into the pickup and rushed down to the river, where the translators had hitched a ride from a river trader boat that had given them a ride from a tiny town downriver.

The diagnosis confirmed that it was an acute case of cerebral malaria. The headaches are a migraine on steroids. Any sound whatsoever penetrates the brain and causes horrible pain that nearly paralyzes the body.

We hurriedly carried her up the steep bank and attempted to make a comfortable place for her to lie inside the pickup bed. The roads in this area are treacherous, and they were now coupled with the heavy rain we had been getting for the last several months, so making it to town without getting stuck would take some serious prayer and driving skills.

We slowly made our way to the hospital and then hastily delivered our linguist friend to the emergency room. The doctor on call that day was very familiar with malaria because he had already treated hundreds and hundreds of people with these very symptoms. His diagnosis of her condition was the same as Betty's earlier assessment, and he immediately began IV treatments. Several days later, our friend regained consciousness and was able to speak a few words before going back to her unconscious state. Her husband and kids were getting plenty of care and prayer support back at the Center but watching Dan's wife and mama to his children in this kind of condition was still excruciatingly worrisome.

After a couple of weeks, she was dismissed from the hospital to recover in the comfort of one of the homes at the Center.

———

By this time, I was already beginning to plan out our next visit to the Paumari tribe. We needed to introduce them to the farming technique of raising chickens, both as a food source and a potential income opportunity.

One afternoon, Dan dropped by to thank us for caring for him and his family. He was enamored with my wife's ability to remain calm during such a moment of crisis, as was I. He went on to say that "we left the village in such a hurry because a riverboat had stopped at our location to see if the

Indians had any jungle product to trade for liquor. Finding our family in desperate need, they agreed to allow us to get on the boat and they would take us to a tiny town in the interior of the Amazon jungle. All I had time to do is load whatever food items we had not yet consumed and I took it up river to our Brazilian friend's storage unit. Would you please take your family and go down into this tribal location and let the Mura Piraha know that my wife will survive? Then, if you would, could you please get the men to work together and clear the airstrip so we can fly in after my wife recovers?"

Betty and I immediately began praying, asking the Lord, "Should we change our own plans and make this visit to the Mura Piraha?"

We had already made several visits to this tribal location, but we had some major reservations. This tribe was one of tangible spiritual darkness. The current translation team was the third family attempting to complete their translation. Every family that went there ended up with unbelievable psychological crises – health wise and emotionally.

The demonic presence was stifling, and most of the tribal communication was filtered through people who were intoxicated with liquor or drugs.

Compared to what we were potentially facing, our plans for going back to the Paumari seemed rather easy.

*Should we stick with our commitment to the Paumari, or do
we go ahead and take on the scary adventure of going to
the Mura Piraha? Lord, please show us!*

For several days Betty and I both had a feeling that He would
be asking us to change our plans: we knew He was going to
call us to the Mura Piraha. Then we received a letter from a
supporting church in Wayne, Michigan. There was a little
handwritten note included:

> "Trust in the Lord to protect you wherever
> He asks you to go and minister.
> We are praying for your family on a daily basis."

There it was.

We had an inexcusably clear indication of what we needed
to do. We quickly began making plans to change course and
planned our visit to the Piraha.

Dan had told us they had stored enough food to last over a
month, so we didn't need to take a lot of provisions. My wife
restocked her medical kit, and I purchased a number of new
machetes to ensure we had an ample supply of them to cut
the airstrip. Within a few short hours, we were ready to go.
This was going to be a LONG trip – we were totally dependent on river trader passages traveling on several rivers to
reach our tribal location.

The next morning, we put on our travel backpacks loaded with whatever leftover food we had in our refrigerator, picked up our children, and went down to the riverbank to wait for a boat to pass. After several hours, we finally thought we saw what looked like a trader boat. We were right – it was definitely a boat. We finally had a way to make the first eight hours of our journey. We waived them in and they very graciously allowed my family to get on board so that we could be on our way to the Piraha.

Sleeping on these boats is surprisingly comfortable. People bring their own hammocks to hang wherever space allows, so it ends up being a pretty decent accommodation as long as the boat is moving. When it stops, though, the mosquitos swarm in and it becomes atrociously uncomfortable.

We arrived at our first destination point, which was where I needed to find a smaller boat that could take us on the next step to our jungle site. Bargaining with cash in my hands always made it much easier to find somebody willing to take us up the river. After talking to several boat owners, I was able to hire one for this leg of the trip which would take up a full day, maybe two. He asked us to wait until the next morning since he would need to purchase fuel to make it to our destination and he could make it back.

Giving cash for these trips was always risky business.

Prior to this trip, I had paid a boatman only to find out he'd taken my cash and consumed the entire amount on a binge at the local bar. So, there we were, desperate to find a place to sleep while trusting this guy to keep his promise to take us to the tribe.

Luckily, we found someone willing to let us sleep in their house. Most of the national Brazilians are very hospitable, especially in the jungle towns. We were like entertainment to them – hosting these weird American missionaries seemed to be some sort of honor to them. Early the next morning, we repacked our few possessions and walked down to the river.

Our boat was there, but nobody was on it. We got on and waited, and waited, and waited. We soon started to think, "My goodness. We got ripped off again! What on earth do we do now?"

Trust me.

That's what kept running through my head, again and again. Late in the morning, we noticed the boat owner stumbling toward us, sitting in his boat. He was obviously inebriated and was going to maneuver this 15' glorified canoe upriver with my precious family onboard. Apparently, he had purchased fuel the night before and was finally ready to take us to the Mura Piraha.

It was another extremely hot jungle day with a constant drizzle, but that was ok with us because it helped us stay somewhat cool while traveling under the tropical sun. Late that evening we arrived at the tribal location. The Piraha Indians

were glad to see us and were happy to hear that the translators were going to be okay and would return later. Because
it was now dark, we crawled up the steep riverbank to hang
our hammocks and fell right to sleep. Our kids were incredibly tired after a long journey of sitting on these rickety boats
– we were all happy to be in a home that was somewhat
protected from the rain that was now pouring out of the sky.

After spending some cultural time reconnecting with the
Piraha, I asked the Chief if I could use his canoe to go check
on the storage place Dan had talked about. Before they left,
Dan had food and supplies stashed there. The Chief was
more than happy to lend me his canoe – they knew I always
paid for their services, either with food or cash.

I left with happiness in my spirit, feeling confident that our
task assignment for this visit wasn't going to be too difficult:
it would only take us a couple of weeks to clear the airstrip.
We made arrangements with the JAARS pilot to come pick
us up in about four weeks, so we had ample time to clear
the brush and jungle regrowth that grows so aggressively
because of the heavy rainfall.

I arrived at the Brazilians' clearing and was delighted to see
that Jaõn was there, which was rather rare. He survived by
hunting and fishing, and most of the time we had been there
previously, he wasn't there, but rather on one of his long hunting trips. His survival was based on hunting and selling skins
to the river traders. He greeted me with a huge smile and gave
me the traditional Brazilian greeting—a major bear hug! We

talked for some time and I knew my wife and children were waiting for my return with the food and clothing supplies.

Another cultural hug and I left to walk over to the storage shed.

When I saw the shed, my spirit of happiness quickly turned to dread. The door had been ripped off and the whole place was empty except for one little jar of mayonnaise and one little bottle of mustard.

Everything was gone.

What in the world were we going to do now? All we had to eat were the leftovers that Betty had put in her backpack. Our children were already hungry from the long boat trip and now we had nothing to give them to eat. The Piraha were also hungry because the heavy rains had raised the water level in the rivers and it's very difficult to catch fish when the water is so high. On top of that, jungle hunting is significantly more difficult in the rainy season. My anxiety levels were raising steadily alongside my blood pressure.

I returned and shared with Betty the situation. Again, we found ourselves in a situation that took major prayer and trust in Jesus. *If only* we could contact the Wycliffe Center back in Porto Velho, then our network of churches and supporters would come to our aid. But we had no radios, no way to contact the outside world. All we had was a direct prayer line to our Heavenly Father.

Jesus, please help us!

When I shared with the Chief my findings at the storage shed, he seemed rather evasive, which caused me to think that perhaps he was involved in the theft. This language group views stealing differently than we do in American culture. In their culture, if you are not using whatever I need at that moment, I have the right to take it – it's not stealing. I wonder if that is exactly what the thieves had been thinking when they knew the translator family had taken food to the storage unit and just left it! Apparently, they didn't need it, but we do.

The very same people we had come to serve – to help – had just placed my family in a potentially terrible circumstance. The Piraha are always hungry, many of them sick with malaria. Betty was treating them as best she could, but both of us were starting to question our decision to change plans and come to this God-forsaken location. I know we're commanded in the Scripture to love the unlovable, but Lord, *give me a break.*

Without even realizing it, we found ourselves developing a very bitter attitude. Satan was infecting our hearts and attitudes toward these people. I would see the Piraha lounging around our little hut and I found myself repulsed by them.

Get me out of here.

Our kids were crying and fussing, my relationship with Betty was under a lot of stress: we needed to get on our knees and ask the Lord to change us. We needed Him to command power over our emotions and physical needs.

It's not like we heard any voices -- the clouds didn't part -- but I did get an idea:

Get up – stop feeling sorry for yourself. Pray for the Piraha. Pray that they would be able to catch fish to feed their families, that maybe they'd have a little extra to feed your own family. Get up – you have work to do. Get a group together and start clearing that airstrip.

Betty and I invited the Chief and his wife over to our house to join us while we prayed for our situation. We spoke in Portuguese – our attempts to speak the Mura Piraha language were less than eloquent. The Chief and his wife didn't have any semblance of a relationship with the Lord, nor did they care to develop one. But we knew we were called to use every possible situation to model our spiritual relationship with Jesus to them. We couldn't squander any opportunity to bring Jesus into their lives.

We finished praying and asked them to share with his people that we had just prayed that they would begin catching fish and maybe even have a successful hunt to feed their families. I then asked the Chief to arrange a crew of 10 – 15 men to begin clearing the airstrip. He wasn't all that excited to share either of those requests with his people but he reluctantly agreed.

Nothing happened that evening. We ate our meal and went on with our lives for the night: we were still rationing the last of our "leftovers," which were now covered with mustard and mayonnaise.

Yuck.

When I talked to the Chief, I had asked him to relay to the tribe that I needed 10-15 men to help me clear the 10,000 feet or so of grass and brush that was overgrown. There were also about 3,000 additional feet of trees that were growing rapidly as a result of the heavy rainfall over the past few months. There was a lot to do, so I needed a lot of help.

Four men showed up that morning.

There was no fathomable way such a small crew of guys would be able to get all of that work done before the JAARS pilot would come back to pick us up. The guys who did show up were at least excited about our task at hand: they were glad to work with the new machetes I brought and they knew I'd be paying them for their help.

We worked for several hours and decided it was finally time to go back to our little hut and get some cool water to drink. The temperature that day was likely around 120 degrees with absolutely no breeze – it was horrendously hot and humid.

After resting for a short bit, I was motivating myself to get these guys back out there to cut for another three or four hours when suddenly I heard the jungle signal from the Indians. My family still uses this signal: it's a hoot that penetrates all of the jungle noise for very long distances and the Indians used it to tell the tribe that they were approaching the village.

The source was a couple of Piraha Indians who had left early that morning to fish in hopes that they would be able to feed their crying families. Once they were in screaming distance, they kept shrieking, "We caught a fish! We caught a fish!" I've never seen anyone get this excited about catching a fish, but this catch was special.

Immediately, the women hurriedly gathered twigs and wood to build a fire to roast the fish. As the guys crawled up the riverbank into viewing distance, I was shocked. They really had caught a big fish, one big enough for everybody to get at least a couple of bites. The tribe erupted in conversation, the jungle humming with their symphony of excitement. The Mura Piraha language is tonal, so it sounds like they're singing instead of talking to each other.

Our attention quickly shifted away from focusing on our clean-up task – my family was longing to chew on something that wasn't slathered in mustard. The Chief spoke to his tribe. Of course, we didn't understand a single word, but the response indicated to us that he was giving us credit for the men catching a fish. Apparently, he had shared with them that the American couple had talked to a spirit and, as a result, they were granted a meal to enjoy. He then asked us to come take the first piece of the roasted fish.

Personally, I'm not a huge fan of fish. But this fish? This one was special and I savored every delicious bite of it. We took very small portions for ourselves and our children and thanked the Chief profusely for so generously sharing the fish with us. It didn't take very long before the fish was completely devoured by the members of the tribe.

That night, we did our best to explain to them that it wasn't us who had allowed them to catch the fish, but that the Almighty Heavenly Father had answered our prayer and had granted the ability to land the fish. They probably didn't understand a single word of what we were trying to say in our broken attempts at conversing with them in their native tongue, but it was obvious that we had gained a level of respect from them.

The hunger came back the next morning, but we felt it was imperative that we keep moving forward with our task of clearing the airstrip. The four guys who had helped the day before were joined by a couple more men from the tribe, and we began working bright and early to beat the terrible heat that would soon return.

I found myself praying aloud in English while I was swinging my machete. Because of the language barrier, I had complete and total privacy.

Lord, thank you for answering our prayer yesterday.
We are so dependent on You, and
You promised never to forsake us.
We need your provision and protection
in this depressing place.
Please give us your love and appreciation for
this group of people under evil oppression.

Time passed quickly as I was working and praying – I was in a sort of spiritual trance. Eventually, one of the guys interrupted my stupor to beg for a break: it was already time to cool off.

While we were resting, I could hear the guys telling their families that the American was talking to someone in another language *again*. They had no idea that I had been praying. Apparently, whatever they were saying to each other was working: several guys came up to me to ask if I had a machete for them to use so they could help clear the airstrip. It was astonishing – maybe the Lord was answering my pleading prayer.

All of the machetes I had brought in were bring used, plus we had additional men who could rotate and carry the cut grass and shrubs off to the side. Finishing the first 500 feet that day was incredible – it was astonishing what a difference having a full squad of volunteers made.

That night, we were again greeted with that glorious jungle hoot. A couple of the guys had gone fishing after working on the airstrip all day and had caught more fish. In the pitch-black jungle darkness, people were scrambling around again to light a fire. Unlike last time, there was enough fish for everyone to take several bites instead of just one. The Chief joyously delivered us a whole roasted fish on a banana leaf. Our stomachs were filled with nourishing food – and mustard was nowhere to be found.

The Lord was turning a terrible food shortage situation around right in front of our eyes. Not only were they able to catch fish to eat that night, but they brought so many fish to the village that we were hanging them in the trees to dry so we could eat them later. The Lord had heard our plea. The clearing crew was continuing to grow and the attitude of the Mura Piraha was changing in a major way. The Chief was continuing to think it was somehow our power that had allowed his people to catch these fish, and I kept insisting that *no*, it was not us. We had nothing to do with it – Jesus was blessing his people. We were approximately at the halfway point of clearing the strip when the Chief asked me to join him on a fishing trip after work. I was excited that he would ask and responded with a quick, "Let's go!"

Several of the other guys wanted to join us, so we loaded into some small two-person canoes, which were just large logs with the meat carved out of them. While we were out catching fish, the women were back at the village preparing for our return. By now, it was an expectation that we would return with a lot of fish for them to enjoy that night.

While the women were waiting back at the village, Betty was attempting to interact with them and build up her Piraha communication skills. Suddenly, they heard the sound of a single engine motor pushing a boat toward their village location: river traders. These river traders would often stop by and see if they could bargain for food or jungle product by paying with liquor.

These were NOT good men. A lot of these guys would abuse and assault the women during these stops, which was something this particular village hadn't been immune to. Hearing the sound of their engine brought back a lot of terrible and painful memories for these women whom Betty was cultivating relationships with. They huddled around her and begged her to protect them.

All of the Piraha men were gone. There were only wives and young girls in the village right then. Betty really was their only source of hope.

The boat pulled up to the riverbank, toting a falling-down-drunk sailor.

Betty marched her fiery self to the riverbank and raised her little hand in the most powerful way she knew how. "In the name of Jesus, I rebuke you!"

The men stopped dead in their tracks and shielded their eyes with their filthy hands. When they caught sight of the ruckus on the hill, they hurried back to their boats, started their engines, and got the heck out of there.

We later heard that the men had reported seeing an army of men standing on the riverbank, machetes in hand, ready to defend the women. God's power was unmistakable that night on the banks of the Mura Piraha's tribal location.

When we got back from our successful fishing trip, the tribe was already buzzing about what had transpired while we were gone. Everyone was gathered around the fire to discuss the incredible events of the day. What had started as a very depressing trip had quickly changed into a splendid time of change at this tribal location.

However, we were rapidly approaching the four-week mark and the strip still wasn't finished. The guys were tired; the machetes were well-worn. Most of the guys had developed calluses on their hands from swinging the machetes for so many hard hours. As each day passed, the pressure mounted for us to get our job done. But somehow, someway, by the night before our JAARS pilot was scheduled to make the 2 ½ hour flight to our village, we were short only by about 30 yards.

Exhausted, but exhilarated, I crawled into my hammock that night and replayed our visit in my head. Betty was softly singing and praying right next to me and I was completely overwhelmed by the Lord's love and provision for us. It was like we were in the Awesome and Holy presence of the powerful name of Jesus. Our kids were sleeping soundly, their little bellies filled to the brim with fish. We had just experienced a jungle rendition of the "feeding of the 5,000" miracle from the Gospels.

The next morning the plane was scheduled to arrive and land on the airstrip we had worked so hard at clearing. I was still a little worried that our efforts would fall short – that he wouldn't have quite enough room. We didn't complete the required distance, but hopefully we had cleared enough so that he could land and take off again.

Our whole crew got up early that morning and hustled to clear the remaining patch of unkempt runway. There was electricity in the air – we were ALL excited. I had asked the pilot to bring some supplies for the Piraha when he came back and I knew Dan was back at the Center purchasing gunpowder, fishhooks, clothing, canned sardines, and the ever-coveted Spam.

Of course, Betty and I were eager to share how the Lord had protected us and had provided for our physical needs on this trip. We couldn't wait to tell our fellow missionaries how the trip we had been desperate to avoid had turned into an experience filled with unforgettable miracles.

Mid-morning, we heard the sound of the Cessna 206. There's really nothing like it when you've been isolated out in the middle of the jungle. I could hear Betty and the kids *hooting and hollering* with excitement. The crew and I immediately dropped our machetes and sprinted to the approach end of the airstrip. Betty had already beat us there with our children. We were so excited – literally breathless in our anticipation. In near perfect unison, we all started screaming, "I see it! I see it!"

The pilot started his safety check circling the airstrip. This was usual: they have to assess the safety of where they are about to land. This time, though, he was circling multiple times. I was standing there thinking to myself,

What's wrong? Did we not clear enough space?
Did he see some kind of danger we didn't?

On his third flyover, he got really low, but it was obvious he still wasn't going to land. I could see into the aircraft at this point and was shocked to see someone sitting in the co-pilot seat. Did he not realize that this plane was *just* big enough to carry my family? There wasn't room for a passenger and my entire family.

My excitement fell to despair: here we go again, another disaster. What else could possibly go wrong on this trip? The pilot made one last approach and finally landed his Cessna safely on our airstrip, using every last inch of the area we had cleared. He turned the plane around and taxied it back to the entry point where we were all waiting.

He shut down the engine and opened his door to an irate missionary brother. I didn't recognize the passenger, I only heard the pilot say that a new short-term missionary had just arrived in Porto Velho to serve as a teacher for missionary kids living at the Center. Absolutely frustrated, I confronted the pilot. "How do you expect to fly out my family and this random passenger in one flight without an extra seat?"

The pilot quickly assured me that they already had a plan: he was going to make two flights that day. The guest was planning to stay at the village while the pilot flew us all back to Porto Velho. While he was there, he was also going to grab another load of supplies from Dan.

Yet again, what seemed to be another crisis ended up being a double blessing for the Mura Piraha. I asked my crew to finish up the last part of the uncleared airstrip while the plane was en route for the next leg of their plan.

As the plane took off, we all found ourselves with tears in our eyes. It had been a trying, difficult, sometimes terrifying four weeks here, but it had also been a life-changing experience. The Lord is so faithful and we are so weak and needy. I was shocked by how quickly my selfishness kicked back into gear when I saw that passenger on *my* plane. How dare that guy piggyback off of the flight I had ordered and paid for? But this change of plans had provided an amazing opportunity for this new missionary. He was able to experience first-hand what the ministry of Wycliffe is all about while he got to spend about six hours working next to the Piraha to clear the last few meters of the airstrip. On top of that, he had also paid for our flight and his.

God, forgive me for being so quick to judge others.

Back at the Center, Dan and his family were still recovering slowly – the key word being "recovering." His wife still needed several months to gain enough strength to return to their tribal location. In the meantime, Dan was still able to return to the location to keep the airstrip maintained. Air travel really does beat trying to hitch a ride on the river.

———

Oh Lord, I pray for the person reading this right now. Perhaps they are in a similar situation today: feeling alone and not experiencing a quick answer to prayer. Lord, please cover them with your grace and mercy and meet their needs through your incredible love and sufficiency.

XVIII
Betty's Trip to Heaven

For several years, Betty had been saying she wanted to ride the narrow-gauge train from Durango to Silverton in Colorado. On our 38th wedding anniversary, I decided it was time to make that dream come true. I bought my bride the best seat money could buy and we set out on our marvelous adventure.

The weather gave us a mix of every season: hot when we left Kansas, rainy in Denver, cold and windy in Durango, more rain on the train, and finally back to the hot, dry, Kansas summer winds. We had a ludicrously good time on this trip, savoring every minute we had together on our escapade.

When we were driving home – it was a Tuesday morning – Betty got awfully restless and had some trouble breathing, but we didn't think too much about it since we had just gone through a sudden altitude change as we came down through the mountain passes. That night she had some discomfort that acted like heartburn, but a couple of Rolaids seemed to clear it up.

But even though Betty seemed to be fine, something felt *off.*

August 5

I felt strongly in my spirit that she needed to go ahead and make an appointment with her doctor. She went to Moundridge (a nearby hospital) at 8:30 a.m. that Friday. Before I left for work that morning, I asked her to please call me when she got out of her appointment.

Ten o'clock rolled by and I still hadn't heard from her. I was starting to feel uneasy.

Around 11:00 a.m. she finally called me. In a calm voice she said, "Dean, I've had a heart attack," and immediately broke down into sobs.

At that point, the doctor took the phone, "We're putting her in an ambulance and taking her to Promise Hospital in Hutchinson."

I immediately jumped into my car to be with my sweet bride. I hurried so fast that I beat the ambulance to the hospital. They took her straight into Intensive Care and, within a few minutes, had started the process of putting in a heart catheter.

Thirty long minutes later, the doctor walked out to the waiting room to talk to me. My Betty had three blocked arteries. They scheduled a heart bypass surgery for that next Monday morning.

I called our kids and they were dumbfounded.

Joshua and his family lived in the Inman community, so they were close enough to be there immediately. My other kids, though, were not as geographically fortunate: Duane and his family were all the way down in Kerrville, Texas, Cheyenne and his family were all the way out in Lake Forest, California and Celea and her family were in Huntington Beach, California.

Our kids in California immediately started making plans to fly into Wichita, but the earliest flight they could get was landing around lunchtime on Sunday. Joshua, Sarah, and their four girls all came to the hospital right away and stayed with me.

That Friday evening was probably the most extraordinary time of my life. Betty was on her game: funny, witty, and buoyantly happy. She was hungry after fasting in preparation for her medical exam, so she asked me to go get her a salad from Wendy's. The hospital nurse overheard us talking and reminded us that "we have a tray for her whenever she wants it."

They brought the plate in and, in her straightforward way, Betty stated, "This isn't food. Please get me something I can enjoy."

The kids offered to run down to the cafeteria to find her something she'd like. And, of course, *Red Hots* for dessert. Betty and I were sitting alone in her room and we noticed a couple of vanilla wafers and juice sitting on her tray. She said, "Let's have communion, Dean!"

I will forever treasure that time with her, sharing our last communion meal together.

She was incredibly happy and was feeling great. At about 10 p.m., the doctor came in and told us they were moving her upstairs because there was no reason for her to stay in Intensive Care. Joshua and the girls had already headed home and I called Duane to tell him he should hold up on driving up since Betty was doing great. He had just started a new job as a high school defensive football coach down in Texas and his boss really wanted him to stay for at least the first two weeks of training.

After the kids left, Betty and I prayed together. We both decided I should head home and get a little bit of sleep. Betty was mostly concerned about me remembering to bring her laptop back with me in the morning because she didn't want to fall behind on any of her assignments. She had just started a Faculty Training Course so she could qualify for a teaching position in one of Central Christian College of Kansas' online degree programs.

We were both at perfect peace as I left the hospital that night.

August 6

I woke up with a jolt at about 4:00 that morning. I sensed an incredible urgency to get up and feed the animals and get the goats milked. I sprinted outside and finished those chores in record time. The second I walked in the door, my cell phone rang.

It was the hospital. "Come quickly. Betty is experiencing intense discomfort."

I called Joshua and sped back to the hospital. If you push it, that 15-mile drive from Inman to Hutch Promise Hospital only takes 11 minutes. It didn't take me a second longer than that to make it back to my bride.

I sprinted to the ICU. Betty was screaming – horrible, agonizing screams.

The doctors and nurses were floating around the room like they were performing some sort of intricate dance. They nimbly guided themselves around each other, never missing a step or wasting a second, calmly prepping her for emergency surgery.

I asked a nurse to please call my family, my siblings, our Pastor Alden Dick, my boss, Hal Hoxie, and his wife, Kathy, and my co-workers. I begged her to ask them to pray.

Joshua, his family, and Pastor Alden all arrived and we huddled together. Praying. Trying desperately to come to grips with what was going on.

It was about two hours before the doctor finally emerged. "I'm so sorry, I'm so sorry."

He just kept repeating it.

I went numb.

The speed and dexterity with which they prepared her for surgery was gone. They slowly wheeled her down that long, sterile hallway back to her bed in ICU. They brought her back from that cold – so bitterly cold – room.

We went back into the ICU room to spend some alone time with her. She wasn't responsive but it was important that we do this, no matter how devastating it felt to be there.

Pretty soon, our friends started showing up to the hospital to pray and to support me and my family. Our neighbors, John and Lorraine Flaming, came up with their son, Scott. For some reason or another, Scott wouldn't leave the room. He stood quietly in the back, ceaselessly praying. Sometimes out loud, sometimes only mouthing his plea to God, all the while stalking the computer monitors for any sign of movement.

He stayed with me every moment of the day and through that night until my kids arrived. Then he stoically stood in the doorway, softly covering my family in prayer. His gentle kindness touched me deeply; it was obvious that he was appointed by the Lord to comfort me in prayer during those long, agonizing hours.

After Betty had been back in ICU for about an hour, her blood pressure started to come up. She still wasn't responsive, but my heart fluttered with the hope that maybe, just maybe, her little heart was responding to my pleas. I was begging for her to hang on – at least until our kids got there. "Betty, hang on. The kids are coming as fast as they can. They've boarded the plane and will be here soon. Please, just hang on."

I ran out to the waiting room to tell my praying friends that the pressure indicators were elevating. It was slight, but it was *something*. "Please, don't stop praying!"

That Saturday was the longest day and night of my life. Sarah sweetly sang hymn after hymn at Betty's bedside, even through a good part of the night. Joshua and I tried to sing along with her, but how can you sing while weeping? While watching the computer screens, the nurse started gently singing with us. His compassion for us became so special to me as the nurse, but also the caregiver for this difficult time of seeing my wife's life slip away.

Betty's heart was artificially pumping blood, but the pressure failed to come up significantly and the indicators weren't reading any continued improvements. By then, we had a lot of friends and co-workers with us at the hospital – a lot of them stayed and prayed all night.

August 7

Pastor Alden stopped by Sunday morning before he went to preach. He prayed for us in the ICU, and he prayed with those incredible friends gathered in the waiting area. I will never stop being grateful for those wonderful people who spent hours upon hours covering my family in prayer.

By about 1:00 p.m. the other kids finally made it. They flew all night, from LA to several other cities before they finally got to Wichita, Kansas. A friend of Joshua agreed to pick them up at the airport. Cheyenne and I were on the phone basically the entire time they drove the 50 miles from the Wichita airport to Hutchinson as we pled with the Lord to let Betty stay with us until they got there.

The Lord kindly answered these prayers. When they were about five miles from the hospital, Joshua and I hurried outside to meet them. Every one of us sprinted back to her room.

We all wept and prayed. We expressed our love and they tried their best to say goodbye.

It ripped my heart out to see my kids and grandkids reluctantly force themselves to let go of Betty's hand.

The doctor and I had discussed that morning how we wanted to navigate the waters of pulling Betty's life support. I was adamant that we wait for my whole family to get there before we made the decision, and the staff willingly honored my request.

After everyone said their goodbyes, we called Duane and, all together, we decided to go ahead and disconnect the life support systems. Betty and I had made this decision years ago, vowing not to keep each other alive on life support while we were dying.

The doctor stood there, full of the most gracious respect, while we made the most devastating decision I've ever had to make. He calmly asked us to leave the room and wait outside of the doorway while they disconnected the system.

He came back moments later and gently ushered me into the room alone. Betty's soul left the ICU in less than thirty seconds. When I saw her lifeless body, I fully understood II Corinthians 5:6-8:

Therefore, we are always confident and know that as long as we are at home in the body we are away from the Lord. For we live by faith, not by sight. We are confident, I say, and would prefer to be away from the body and at home with the Lord.

My beautiful bride had lost her luster, her body was just a hollow shell of what it used to be. Betty's faith had become sight and she was present with the Lord. The vitality she always brought into the world was now in Heaven.

What had been a busy, loud room immediately turned into a cold, lifeless mortuary. When they shut off those machines, Betty's soul left this earth, and it was like the last bit of warmth had left with her.

I asked the rest of the family to come back into the room and we wept, holding onto each other for some kind of support while we tried to fathom our loss. It took a long time before I could make that dreary walk out to the waiting room to let our friends – those magnificent prayer warriors – know that my Betty was dancing in Heaven.

A few hours after her death, the Lord painted a Kansas sunset like no other. Betty loved to paint clouds on canvas – a talent she had just started to enjoy in her last years of life – and as we stood in our yard basking in this glorious sunset, it was as if the Lord was telling us that He and Betty were painting it just for us. We marveled at His awesome painting and thanked Jesus for that little piece of comfort.

After

I spent the next several days in shock. I was heartbroken, lost, and lonely without my vivacious Betty. I was feeling completely and totally out of it. My kids were great at supporting each other – and me. Duane arrived as quickly as he could, no matter what that head coach wanted, and we started arranging the burial and memorial service.

In everything we've ever done, Betty and I have always liked to do things our own way. Betty's memorial service was no different. We planned an early morning burial, followed by a memorial service at our church where we sang songs of worship to our loving heavenly Father who now had the joy of holding my bride in His arms.

We had friends show up from as far as the West Coast, Houston, and all over the Midwest. This was probably the longest service ever in the history of Bethel Mennonite Church, but we didn't care. We weren't going to be rushed by the clock. We needed to spend time worshipping him as best as we could until our hearts had healed enough to leave that sanctuary.

———

My heart aches to be with her again, but until that time I stand on the promise of Zephaniah 3:17:

The Lord your God is with you, the Mighty Warrior who saves.
He will take great delight in you;
in his love he will no longer rebuke you,
but will rejoice over you with singing.

Afterword

Vivid, real-life, survivor-type experiences presented in a very personal and touching way. The words truly seem to pour from Dean's heart.

Filled with stories of complete and utter trust (and dependence) in the Lord their God.

The stories within this book are communicated so personally and with a tenderness that represents Dean's nature and his walk with God, and at the same time demonstrate remarkable toughness, courage and persistence that will challenge the reader.

It quickly becomes obvious that Dean, Betty and their family truly did go through the experiences highlighted in this book. The words are alive, personal and descriptive of their generous hearts, physical and mental toughness, and commitment to underserved people. Their dedication and "all in" attitude toward building trust and working relationships with others less fortunate is significant, powerful and challenging.

Dean accomplished his goal of recording and communicating special, precious times shared as a family that is indeed a legacy of hope, trust and courage. Furthermore, the challenge to grasp the incredible truth of God's love for each and all becomes obvious.

There is no doubt that Dean and Betty were true partners in the adventure of serving throughout their lives, and that reality becomes most apparent in their Brazilian experiences. Truly a blessing to have a glimpse into what a beloved partnership completely committed God's call accomplished through Dean and Betty.

The stories in this book are strong evidence of Dean and Betty's complete and utter trust in God, His Word and their very personal relationships with Him provide a significant challenge for each of us (the reader). The trust they demonstrated daily for absolutely everything (including their entire family!) is extraordinary and remarkable.

Dean has shared experiences that indicate extreme commitment, sacrifice beyond most imaginations, and flat-out challenges to some of us – what are our loves that God might be challenging us to leverage for others and His kingdom?

The book is a heart-warming snapshot into some very personal accounts of what two individuals totally committed to the Lord and to each other can accomplish together. Their stories show what it can mean when we embrace who we are and allow our uniqueness to be available for God.

Enjoyable and difficult to put down.

Dr. Gary Anderson

Andy Addis is a pastor, leader, motivational speaker/trainer and author. Primarily, Andy claims his most important roles are Christian, husband and father.

During the last decade Andy has spoken and lead conferences like ADVANCE Leadership, Super Summer Youth Camps, Fellowship of Christian Athletes events, and Christian Challenge College Conferences.

Andy is the author of two books: Reading It Right and BLOTCH.

Andy is married to Kathy and they have two wonderful boys: Noah (age 17) and Nathan (age 15).

Dr. Gary Anderson is a prominent veterinarian in the state of Kansas. He is also a great friend and colleague of Dr. Kroeker.

Dr. Dean Kroeker grew up in a rural community Inman Kansas, and began his professional life working in sales and management for Fruehauf Trailer Corporation. This experience prepared him to serve as a missionary with Wycliffe Bible Translators (WBT-Community Development Specialist) working nine years in the Amazon jungle of Brazil and an additional fourteen years at the Mission Headquarters in Huntington Beach, California.

After returning to the U.S., he completed a Bachelor of Science degree at Biola University, Masters in Management from National University and completed a Doctor of Education degree in Organizational Leadership from Pepperdine University.

Dr. Kroeker founded a 501 C-3 non-profit counseling center, (Springboard Ministry), specifically dedicated to serve the economically challenged population in Southern California. Currently he is employed at Central Christian College of Kansas in McPherson, Kansas, where he has served as Faculty, Administrator, Dean of Professional and Distance Education, Special Assistant to the President, and is currently the V.P of Advancement and Alumni Relations.